Food for the Journey:

The Biblical Roots of the La Salette Message
Volume One

By

Fr. Normand Theroux, M. S.

Missionaries of La Salette Corporation
915 Maple Avenue
Hartford, CT 06114-2330, USA

Website: www.lasalette.org

Copyright © September 19, 2017 by Missionaries of Our Lady of La Salette, Province of Mary, Mother of the Americas, 915 Maple Avenue, Hartford, CT, 06106-2330, USA

Imprimi Potest:

Rev. Fr. René J. Butler, M.S., Provincial Superior
Missionaries of Our Lady of La Salette,
Province of Mary, Mother of the Americas
915 Maple Avenue
Hartford, CT 06106-2330, USA

All rights reserved. No part of this book may be reproduced, stored in a retrieval system, or transmitted, in any form or by any means, electronic, mechanical, photocopying, recording or otherwise, without the written permission of La Salette Communications Center Publications, 947 Park Street, Attleboro, MA 02703 USA

Scripture texts in this work are taken from the New American Bible with Revised New Testament and Revised Psalms © 1991, 1986. 1970 Confraternity of Christian Doctrine, Washington, D.C. and are used by permission of the copyright owner. All Rights Reserved. No part of the New American Bible may be reproduced in any form without permission in writing from the copyright owner.

Printed in the United States of America

We are most grateful to Fr. Normand Theroux, M.S., for his generosity in entrusting his La Salette materials to us for publication.

Editor and author of "For Your Reflection" : Fr. Ron Gagne, M.S.

Booklet Design and Digital Formatting: Jack Battersby and Fr. Ron Gagne, M.S.

This and other La Salette titles are available in paper, e-book and audiobook formats at: www.Amazon.com and itunes.Apple.com, www.Lasalette.org

ISBN: 978-1-946956-11-8

Contents

An Introduction: Setting the Scene   1
Prologue: The Story of the La Salette Apparition 14

Part One: Conversion
Chapter One: La Salette-A Sign of New Times-New Beginnings 22
Chapter Two: The Man Who Lived the Truth   25
Chapter Three: What Faith in God Means   28
Chapter Four: When Concern is Hard to Kill   32
Chapter Five: A Question of Authority   36
Chapter Six: There is Always a Reason Not to Dance   40

Part Two: Called to Do God's Will
Chapter Seven: Proceeding in Haste   45
Chapter Eight: Blessed Be the Lord   49
Chapter Nine: To the Childlike   53
Chapter Ten: That Big, Strong Gospel Keystone 56

Part Three: The Generosity of the Cross
Chapter Eleven: Repaid in Secret   61
Chapter Twelve: "In Remembrance of Me"   65
Chapter Thirteen: Blood and Water   68
Chapter Fourteen: The Joy of the Bridegroom   72

Part Four: God's Compassion, Mercy, and Healing
Chapter Fifteen: The Lord of Life and Burdens Light   76
Chapter Sixteen: Believing Because He Saw   79
Chapter Seventeen: The Blind Men Who Caught Up to Christ   83
Chapter Eighteen: The Reign of God is Here   86

Part Five: Love and Service
Chapter Nineteen: Portrait of the Neighbor   91
Chapter Twenty: I Do Not Wish to Send Them Away Hungry   94
Chapter Twenty-One: The Waters of Life   98
Chapter Twenty-Two: When Words Become Flesh and Blood   102

Part Six: Life, Death, and New Life
Chapter Twenty-Three: The Bold Advances of a Loving God   107
Chapter Twenty-Four: The Joy of Living 111
Chapter Twenty-Five: The Dying of Death   115

An Introduction:

Setting the Scene

by Fr. Flavio Gillio, M.S.

Fr. Flavio Gillio M.S.

I have never personally met Fr. Normand Theroux, M.S. and yet we have become good friends. Whenever I have a chance to visit his gravesite in the small cemetery the Shrine of Our Lady of La Salette in Enfield, New Hampshire, we spend a little time together and we peacefully converse. Yes, I guess we have become good friends. After all, we both share the same passion for the Scripture, we both studied in Rome at the Pontifical Biblical Institute and, more importantly, we have both being seduced by the same "Beautiful Lady"!

I have, therefore, welcomed with joy the invitation to write an introduction to this volume, *Food for the Journey; the Biblical Roots of the La Salette Message, Volume One*. Fr. Theroux's own title for this collection evokes one of the most used biblical metaphors to unfold the hidden meaning of our own lives – that of a journey or pilgrimage.

We are on a Journey

Bible stories constantly remind us that the idea of "journey" or "pilgrimage" bears a deeply interconnected anthropological and theological value. On the one hand, we are and belong to a pilgrim people, to a pilgrim community. On the other hand, we do not walk alone. Like the pilgrim community of Israel in the desert, we are found by the One for whom we are searching: the God of Abraham, Isaac, Jacob, the Father of Jesus, the Messiah.

God introduces himself as a pilgrim God, looking for his wandering people. It is not a coincidence that one the greatest modern Jewish thinkers, philosophers and theologians, Abraham Joshua Heschel, entitled one of his most known books, *God in Search of Man: A Philosophy of Judaism*. And for us Christians, God's pilgrimage reaches its highest point in Jesus of Nazareth, as Saint John Paul II reminds us in his 1999 letter, *On Pilgrimage*.

The Biblical History of Salvation, from Genesis to Revelation, is conceived as a progressing and unfolding journey from the Paradise lost to the Paradise found. In between, we find a great number of characters who embarked on challenging journeys, both physical and spiritual: Abraham, a "wandering Aramean" (Deuteronomy 26:5) took the risk of journeying towards an unknown land (Genesis 12:1; 15:17; 17:1); Moses, the greatest prophet, led Israel into a collective pilgrimage (Book of Exodus); Hosea, who prophesied to the Northern Kingdom just before the destruction of Israel in 722 B.C., and himself embarked on a painful journey through the ebb and flow of love.

And in the New Testament, a young woman from Nazareth, named Mary, journeyed through the sometimes-dark pilgrimage of raw and heroic faith; Paul and the Apostles, those "pilgrims" for Christ, journeyed from the Torah to the Cross and the resurrected Jesus. They were all men and women "on the way", following and witnessing the One who is the "Way".

This collection of homilies invites us, its readers, to embark on a literary and spiritual journey between two mountains, Mount Sion and the Holy Mountain of La Salette, where the "Beautiful Lady" appeared on September 19, 1846 to two children, Maximin Giraud and Melanie Calvat.

Our guide for this journey is Father Theroux's gentle voice and sharp insight. He allows us to appreciate the height and depth, the width and the length of the many biblical and La Salette landscapes and panoramas that his love for Scripture and for the Beautiful Lady are able to decipher and unfold. These reflections highlight the deep connection between the Bible – and more specifically the Gospels – and the message delivered by Our Lady at La Salette. And, finally, these perceptive meditations can help us understand better and more deeply the Apparition of Our Lady of La Salette as the most biblical of the major Marian Apparitions.

Mary is a Handmaid

Throughout Fr. Theroux's homilies, Mary is discretely present, a handmaid. She never overshadows her Son, but rather she leads us to him – as in the Gospels and in her words and actions at La Salette. Even if, as Fr. Theroux writes in one of his homilies, Mary remains "in obscurity throughout almost the entire New Testament", she keeps on being a discreet but significant presence. Like in the Gospels, so on the Holy Mountain of La Salette, Mary's presence is simply and entirely Christ-centered:

"The crucifix on the Lady's breast at La Salette is more than a symbol. (Jesus) is the 'Son' she mentions three times in her discourse. He is the center of her life. He is her life. She had given him his body, his humanity. She had given him the blood he had shed on Calvary. The Lady who had stood on Calvary now stands at La Salette. She was called 'mother' on Calvary and this was to prove more than a title. She weeps still up to this very day for all her people and

Madonna By Lorenzo Costa

for each one of them."

Regarding Mary's discrete but significant presence in her Son's life, the *Dogmatic Constitution on the Church, Lumen Gentium*, one of the principal documents of the Second Vatican Council, points out:

> *"In the public life of Jesus, Mary makes significant appearances. This is so even at the very beginning, when at the marriage feast of Cana, moved with pity, she brought about by her intercession the beginning of miracles of Jesus the Messiah. In the course of her Son's preaching she received the words whereby in extolling a kingdom beyond the calculations and bonds of flesh and blood, he declared blessed those who heard and kept the word of God, as she was faithfully doing.*
>
> *"After this manner the Blessed Virgin advanced in her pilgrimage of faith, and faithfully persevered in her union with her Son unto the cross, where she stood, in keeping with the divine plan, grieving exceedingly with her only begotten Son, uniting herself with a maternal heart with his sacrifice, and lovingly consenting to the immolation of this Victim which she herself had brought forth. Finally, she was given by the same Christ Jesus dying on the cross as a mother to his disciple with these words: 'Woman, behold your son'" (Lumen Gentium, Chapter 8, #58).*

Mary as Prophet and Teacher

While guiding his readers to climb the two mountains, Fr. Normand Theroux paints Mary as prophet, teacher, and tender companion and mother. With the biblical prophets, Mary at La Salette shares the "… grace and terrifying vocation…" of giving voice to someone else's words, demanding to be heard:

> *"At La Salette, Our Lady spoke in the name of her Son. She clearly did not say what she said on her own authority. She reminds people of the Mass, the day, Sunday, reserved for the*

Lord, penance, prayer and respect and honor for the Name of her Son. These are all God-centered commandments and the Lady speaks them on the authority of her Son. She mentions this 'Son' repeatedly throughout the apparition, so that there is no doubt about the origin of her message."

As such, Mary's words at La Salette, are words that are "…riven with truth and the truth in them will not expire", as Fr. Theroux writes commenting on the Gospel. He adds, "At La Salette, (she) is Mary, the Queen of Prophets".

In this first volume, *Food for the Journey: the Biblical Roots of the La Salette Message,* Mary also appears as a teacher and catechist. She teaches us, through Fr. Theroux's meditations, how to cope "well with life and its tough problems", and the path to follow in order to grow in intimacy with the Lord.

Finally, the Beautiful Lady of La Salette also accompanies us on our journey, as a tender and vulnerable companion and mother – a compassionate mother who weeps for all those whom she loves. Hopefully all of us have learned from our own life experiences. I believe that Fr. Theroux is correct when he writes that "caring for people brings its share of pain – joys too, of course, but pain in abundance" – a pain born of love. And likewise, the "Beautiful Lady", out of love for her people, experiences a "…flow of tears that flood the heart and cannot be held back."

Shedding Tears

At La Salette, Mary's tears are not only among those traits that make the Apparition of La Salette the most biblical one among the major Marian apparitions, but they are also a key to understanding the message she delivered to Maximin and Melanie. Like in the Gospels, where Jesus' deeds bring to light his words and vice versa, at La Salette too, Mary's actions and attitudes are deeply connected to her words, and they mutually enlighten each other.

In fact, the authors of the bible are not at all hesitant to show even the most well-known persons in our Salvation History coming to tears. And as ironic as it may appear, men in the bible are seen weeping more than women!

Tears in the Bible

For example, Abraham weeps over the dead body of his beloved wife, Sarah (Genesis 23:2).

Esau weeps at the feet of his father, Isaac, when he realizes that his brother, Jacob, has stolen the blessing from his father (Genesis 27:38).

Joseph the dreamer, the great Prince of Egypt, weeps six times. The first time happens in Genesis, chapter 42, verse 24. A second snapshot of Joseph weeping is also described (Genesis 43:30).

Esau and Jacob by Matthias Stom

Later the narrator portrays Joseph to be even bolder in his expression of emotions: "And he wept so loudly that the Egyptians heard him" (Genesis 45:2). And once the family ties are almost reconciled, Joseph weeps once again (Genesis 45:14).

A similar reaction is found when Joseph is reunited with his father (Genesis 46:27). The last time Joseph weeps is at his father's death (Genesis 50:1). From these instances, we can infer that Joseph was not only a great charismatic and confident leader, but he also had a tender heart and did not hesitate to express his powerful emotion in tears.

Similar to the outstanding prince of Egypt is the greatest King of Israel, David. He wept often, and quietly. But one of his most emotional responses occurred when he saw the dead body of his dearest friend, Jonathan, and the body of Jonathan's father, Saul (2 Samuel 1:12).

Even though our male biblical heroes seem to weep quiet frequently, women are not forgotten. For example, Hannah is not ashamed to express her sadness of heart to her beloved husband, Elkanah, through her frequent tears: "Her husband Elkanah would say to her, 'Hannah, why are you weeping? Why don't you eat? Why are you downhearted? Don't I mean more to you than ten sons?'" (1 Samuel 1:8).

As we shift our attention from the Old Testament to the New Testament, both Jesus and Peter, continue the biblical habit of expressing their feelings through tears! Twice, once in Luke and once in John, Jesus is said to weep. He wept while approaching Jerusalem, probably at the Mount of Olives: "As he drew near, (Jesus) saw the city and wept over it" (Luke 19:41). Then he also wept in seeing the dead body of his very dear friend, Lazarus: "When Jesus saw (Mary of Bethany) weeping and the Jews who had come with her weeping, he became perturbed and deeply troubled, and said, 'Where have you laid him?' They said to him, 'Sir, come and see.' And Jesus wept" (John 11:33-35).

Tears – a Sign of Vulnerability

From a biblical perspective, weeping is not necessarily a sign of weakness but rather can be a sign of tender vulnerability and surrender. Weeping unveils the height, width and depth of our own humanity and heart. Yet, as a culture, many of us are not comfortable disclosing times in our lives when tears came to our eyes. Many among us may even feel embarrassed and ashamed at being seen weeping in public.

Just a small example: oftentimes in confession, if a person confessing begins crying, he or she will often say, "Excuse me, Father…", as if this is a shameful or embarrassing response for them. Such a way of thinking may be rooted in the fact that we have been growing up with the tenet, "never let them see you cry". Or, we might feel that, as a modern, sophisticated person, we believe that crying doesn't accomplish anything and could even expose us even to being more deeply hurt. Perhaps we were taught to control our emotions in order to be seen as strong and competent, especially if we have a leadership role in our community, family or elsewhere.

Tears as a Tender Expression of Love

But this way of looking at tears is certainly not what we see in the Apparition of Our Lady at La Salette. At La Salette, the "Beautiful Lady" becomes alive and real through her tears. For example, when Maximin and Melanie saw her crying, they simply thought it was a peasant woman from the village down in the valley who was running away from her family. Mary at La Salette is not embarrassed to appear vulnerable and expose to us her deepest emotions, through her weeping.

And so, what do her tears mean? The liturgical readings for the Feast of Our Lady of La Salette disclose to us their meaning. In our first reading from the book of Genesis, we hear about the rainbow in the clouds as a welcome reminder of God's covenant with us (Genesis 9:13).

At La Salette, Mary's tears also remind us about the good news of God's love and mercy for his people. They speak to us about her and her son's communion with our broken and wounded world – expressing sorrow mingled with hope for our redemption ("*If they are converted…*"). Her tears make her presence real, showing us her deep communion with the needy people in our world. Fr. Theroux highlights this attitude when he writes:

> *"Mary at La Salette came to imitate her Son in what he had done and to share his mission. She showed the world the suffering of an abandoned Lord. She revealed, if it had to be revealed, that in some mysterious way, God grieves and weeps for people. It is nothing less than stirring to see that at La*

Salette, the Lord wanted to let us know that God, is indeed, caring for his people to the point of tears."

Our Crucified Savior Suffers *With* Us and *For* Us

In our brief gospel for the feast, Jesus is seen nailed to the cross, with Mary and one of his disciples faithfully present. Concerning this tragic scene, Fr. Richard Rohr describes the crucified God as one "who walks with crucified people, and thus reveals and redeems their plight as his own. Jesus is not observing human suffering from a distance, but is somehow in human suffering with us and for us."

"Cristo crucificado" by Diego Velazquez

Similarly, at La Salette, Mary bears, on her breast "the crucified Christ… in bright and shimmering evidence. This is a suffering Christ, who in some way, still bears the burden of the cross. The mother herself says clearly, *"How long a time have I suffered for you!"* Like the Son, the "Beautiful Lady of La Salette" is not observing the broken world from afar, from a distance. Instead she is with us and for us. This shows her desire to suffer with us – *"cum passio"*, "to suffer with" – and her tears indicate both her compassion and mercy. Both the Son and his Mother are burdened with suffering, out of love and for those they love.

Mary's tears at La Salette should awaken in us a sense of gratitude and thanksgiving, leading us to pray with the Psalmist: "O bless the Lord, my soul" (Psalm 103:2). This is because Mary's tears are neither a sign of dismiss nor of judgment.

On the contrary, her tears welcome us; they do not judge us or reproach us; they invite us to come closer to her and allow ourselves to be welcomed by her in the same way that the "Beautiful Lady of La Salette" invited and received the two little peasant children. And the opening words of her message emphasize even more her attitude and posture: *"Come near, my children... do not be afraid...I have great news to tell you."*

This is a picture of what it means to be unconditionally loved. We all hunger and thirst for such an experience. As Richard Rohr describes so well:

> *"This is the kind of experience that we all want, that we all wait for, that we all need. Although we want it from one another and we get it occasionally, there is only One who can be relied upon to always receive us and mirror us perfectly as we are."*

It is really a grace to be able, at least once in our own life, to experience being truly loved – not for what we are able to accomplish; not because of our good reputation; but rather to be loved simply for who we are. It is a transforming grace to experience such a moment of unconditional love. We should appreciate that it can be a transforming grace to be touched and moved by the tears of Our Lady of La Salette.

As Paul reminds us in the second reading, Mary's tears, when we allow them to touch our hearts, are able to recreate us – "a new creation" – to reconcile us, and thereby make us ambassadors of Christ's reconciliation.

She Weeps For Those Who Do Not Deserve Her Tears!

Because of that, the tears that Mary shed at La Salette are a challenging call to direct our compassion, mercy and tenderness to those who live at the margins or peripheries of the Church and our world.

As in 1846, it's very easy to recognize that our contemporary world is still filled with people who weep. They may be responding to natural calamities happening around the world; or perhaps weeping over discrimination because of people's different beliefs, religious values, or sexual orientation; or perhaps they come to tears seeing mistreatment and injustice, within and outside the

Church.

Mary's tears at La Salette are tears for *all* her people – without exclusion or discrimination. And if we delve more deeply into the message, Mary weeps for people who do not deserve her tears! In her own words, she weeps for people who "cannot drive the carts without bringing in my Son's name"; for people who do not go to Mass or, if they go, they do so "only to mock religion"; also for people who, during Lent, "go to the meat market like dogs." In short, she weeps for people who do not deserve her tears!

Weeping Mother of La Salette

Once again, the Mother imitates the Son, as Fr. Theroux very well explains:

> *"At La Salette, Mary said, 'Well, my children, you will make it known to all my people.' By the ministry of Maximin and Melanie, her words would stir the Church but go beyond it to the whole world. The entire world is thus called to faith and life. The gospel of John is predicated on faith, on the belief that the love of God for all people is not something one can understand. Only faith can grasp it. The Lady weeps at La Salette for all the people who do not know the beauty of faith which is an aspect of God's love for people."*

Like her Son, Mary at La Salette wishes to reach out to her own people – where they are and whom they are. What a great lesson, modeling for us what compassion, mercy and tenderness are all about! What a wonderful lesson about how to extend our compassion, mercy and tenderness to the margins and peripheries of our Church and world! The Beautiful Lady of La Salette, appearing in this very remote and marginal place, reaches the neediest people where they are found. She is with them and for them!

An Invitation

This collection of homilies, volume one of *Food for the Journey: the Biblical Roots of the La Salette Message*, is meant to be, like the Eucharistic Bread and Wine, food to nourish a special friendship, and a special relationship, while encouraging us, its readers to take "… advantage of those habits of faith…" which Our Lady of La Salette lists in her message: prayer, Eucharist, Lenten observances, and respect for the name and person of her Son.

We can all be truly grateful for Fr. Normand Theroux's love for Scripture and Our Lady of La Salette; ultimately, they give us the opportunity to walk in the footsteps of the One who is the face of the mercy of the Father and in so doing reaffirm our own discipleship. They give us the opportunity to listen anew to Mary's reconciling message and to be transformed into reconciled reconcilers.

They give us the opportunity to open our hearts to the Father's tenderness, mercy and compassion as reflected by the Son through his Mother so that we can become what she preached. After all, in a single half-hour, Maximin and Melanie had learned to love "the Beautiful Lady of La Salette"! And we certainly have more time than that!

May this first volume of Fr. Normand Theroux's homilies be, as he himself expresses with great hope, a "good way to learn who Mary is, what she does and how she practices the gospel command of love". May we pledge to seek out and be ambassadors of reconciliation *with* and *for* those of her people who live on the margins of our Church and world.

May all her people, in addition to Maximin and Melanie, hear the great news: "*Come near, my children, do not be afraid.*" After all, the message of Our Lady of La Salette is a universal call. In Fr. Normand Theroux's own words: "La Salette gives us the sharp message that someone cares enough to call and call again. To speak. To upbraid. To weep" – all without judgment, dismissal, or discrimination. Enjoy this reflective journey and welcome its call to conversion of heart.

Reflection Questions:
- When have you come to tears over an event or a person?
- Who for you is a person of faith and why?

Prayer:
Mary, Weeping Mother of La Salette, we praise you for your life of deep and lasting faith, echoed in your appearance on the Holy Mountain of La Salette. Your gentle invitation to "Come near" can melt our hearts and open our lives to a deeper love for you and your Son. Your prophetic words express your deep concern for us and our daily lives.

As we travel together with you and your Son on this journey of life, deepen our awareness of our need for the gifts of faith and forgiveness. Help us become true and dedicated ministers of reconciliation, sharing your words of correction, comfort and hope with all your people.

May we always place our trust in your loving Son, who lives with the Father and the Holy Spirit, one God, for ever and ever. **Amen**.

La Salette Invocation:
Our Lady of La Salette, Reconciler of Sinners, pray without ceasing for us who have recourse to you.

Prologue:

The Story of the La Salette Apparition

On Saturday, September 19, 1846, a "Beautiful Lady" appeared to two children, both from Corps, in France Alps: Maximin Giraud, eleven-year-old, and Mélanie Calvat, almost fifteen, who were watching their herds on the slope of Mont Planeau, approximately 6,000 feet in altitude, not far from the village of La Salette. In a little hollow, they suddenly noticed a globe of fire – "as though the sun had fallen on the spot." Within the dazzling light they gradually perceived a woman, seated, her elbows resting on her knees and her face buried in her hands.

The two children discover the seated Weeping Mother

The Beautiful Lady rose, and said to the children in French:

Come closer, my children; don't be afraid. I am here to tell you great news.

She took a few steps towards them. Maximin and Mélanie, reassured, ran down to her and stood very close to her.

The Beautiful Lady wept all the time she spoke. She was tall, and everything about her radiated light. She wore the typical garb of the women of the area: a long dress, and apron around her waist, a shawl crossed over her breast and tied behind her back, and a close-fitting bonnet. Along the hem of her shawl she wore a broad, flat chain, and from a smaller chain around her neck there hung a large crucifix. Under the arms of the cross there were, to the left of the figure of Christ, a hammer, and, to the right, pincers. The radiance of the entire apparition seemed to emanate from this crucifix, and shone like a brilliant crown upon the Beautiful Lady's head. She wore garlands of roses on her head, around the edge of her shawl and around her feet.

The Beautiful Lady spoke to the two shepherds. first in French, in these words:

Mary stands and speaks to the children

If my people refuse to submit, I will be forced to let go the arm of my Son. It is so strong and so heavy, I can no longer hold it back.

How long a time I have suffered for you! If I want my Son not to abandon you, I am obliged to plead with him constantly. And as for you, you pay no heed!

However much you pray, however much you do, you will never be able to recompense the pains I have taken for you.

I gave you six days to work; I kept the seventh for myself, and no one will give it to me. This is what makes the arm of my Son so heavy. And then, those who drive the carts cannot swear without throwing in my Son's name. These are the two things that make the arm of my Son so heavy.

If the harvest is ruined, it is only on account of yourselves. I warned you last year with the potatoes. You paid no heed. Instead, when you found the potatoes spoiled, you swore, and threw in my Son's name. They are going to continue to spoil, and by Christmas this year there will be none left.

Mélanie was intrigued by the expression, *pommes de terre*. In the local dialect, potatoes were called las truffas. She looked inquiringly at Maximin, but the Beautiful Lady anticipated her question.

Don't you understand, my children? Let me find another way to say it.

Using the local dialect, she repeated what she had said about the harvest, and then went on:

If you have wheat, you must not sow it. Anything you sow the vermin will eat, and whatever does grow will fall into dust when you thresh it.

A great famine is coming. Before the famine comes, children under seven will be seized with trembling and die in the arms of the persons who hold them. The rest will do penance through the famine. The walnuts will become worm-eaten; the grapes will rot.

At this point the Beautiful Lady confided a secret to Maximin, and then to Mélanie. then she went on:

If they are converted, rocks and stones will turn into heaps of wheat, and potatoes will be self-sown in the fields.

Do you say your prayers well, my children?

"Hardly ever, Madam," the two shepherds answered candidly.

Ah, my children, you should say them well, at night and in the morning, even if you say only an Our Father and a Hail Mary when you can't do better. When you can do better, say more.

In the summer, only a few elderly women go to Mass. The rest work on Sundays all summer long. In the winter, when they don't know what to do, they go to Mass just to make fun of religion. In Lent they go to the butcher shops like dogs.

Have you never seen wheat gone bad, my children?

They answered, "No, Madam."

The Beautiful Lady then spoke to Maximin.

But you, my child, surely you must have seen some once, at Coin, with your father. The owner of the field told your father to go and see his spoiled wheat. And then you went, and you took two or three ears of wheat in your hands, you rubbed them together, and it all crumbled into dust. While you were on your way back and you were no more than a half hour away from Corps, your father gave you a piece of bread and said to you: "Here, my child, eat some bread while we still have it this year; because I don't know who will eat any next year if the wheat keeps up like that."

Mary melted into light

"Oh, yes," answered Maximin, "Now I remember. Just then, I didn't remember it."

The Beautiful Lady then concluded, not in dialect but in French:

Well, my children you will make this known to all my people.

Then she moved forward, stepped over the stream, and without turning back she gave the injunction.

Very well, my children make this known to all my people.

The vision climbed the steep path which wound its way towards the Collet (little neck). Then she rose into the air as the children caught up to her. She looked up at the sky, then down to the earth.

Facing southeast, "she melted into light." The light itself then disappeared.

On September 19, 1851, after "a precise and rigorous investigation" of the event, the witnesses, the content of the message, and its repercussions, Philibert de Bruillard, Bishop of Grenoble, pronounced his judgment in a pastoral letter of instruction. He declared that "the apparition of the Blessed Virgin to two shepherds, September 19, 1846, on a mountain in the Alps, located in the parish of La Salette,... bears within itself all the characteristics of truth and that the faithful have grounds for believing it to be indubitable and certain."

In another pastoral letter, dated May 1, 1852, the Bishop of Grenoble announced the construction of a Shrine on the mountain of the apparition, and went on to add:

> "However important the erection of a Shrine may be there is something still more important, namely the ministers of religion destined to look after it, to receive the pious pilgrims, to preach the word of God to them, to exercise towards them the ministry of reconciliation, to administer the Holy Sacrament of the altar, and to be, to all, the faithful dispensers of the mysteries of God and the spiritual treasures of the Church.
>
> "These priests shall be called the Missionaries of Our Lady of La Salette; their institution and existence shall be, like the Shrine itself, and eternal monument, a perpetual remembrance, of Mary's merciful apparition."

The first priests imbued with the spirit of the Apparition and who devoted themselves to the service of the pilgrims, felt from the beginning the call to and the need for religious life. Six of them pronounced their first vows on February 2, 1858, in accordance with their provisional Constitutions, adapted in 1862 to include Brothers. From that time, Fathers and Brothers have constituted one religious family.

Mary's apparition at La Salette is a modern-day reminder of an ancient truth: that Mary constantly intercedes for us before God; that she is the Reconciler of Sinners, calling us back to the message and way of her Son, Jesus.

Reflection Questions:
- What quality do you most admire about Mary's appearance at La Salette?

- When and where did you first hear the message of Our Lady of La Salette?

Prayer:
Mary, Humble Maiden, your message and witness on the Mountain of La Salette is that of a true reconciler. You invite us to draw near, you speak to our hearts and then you send us off to spread your message of faith, forgiveness and good news to all your people.

La Salette Shrine on the Holy Mountain in France

As Mother of the Church, you are concerned about our daily life with its challenges and blessings. In your goodness, assist us in our journey of faith; guide us with your loving presence and assure us of your Son's grace as we make our way together, back to the Father. We ask this through your intercession, and in the name of your Son, Jesus, who lives with the Father and the Holy Spirit, one God, fore ever and ever. **Amen**.

La Salette Invocation:
Our Lady of La Salette, Reconciler of Sinners, pray without ceasing for us who have recourse to you.

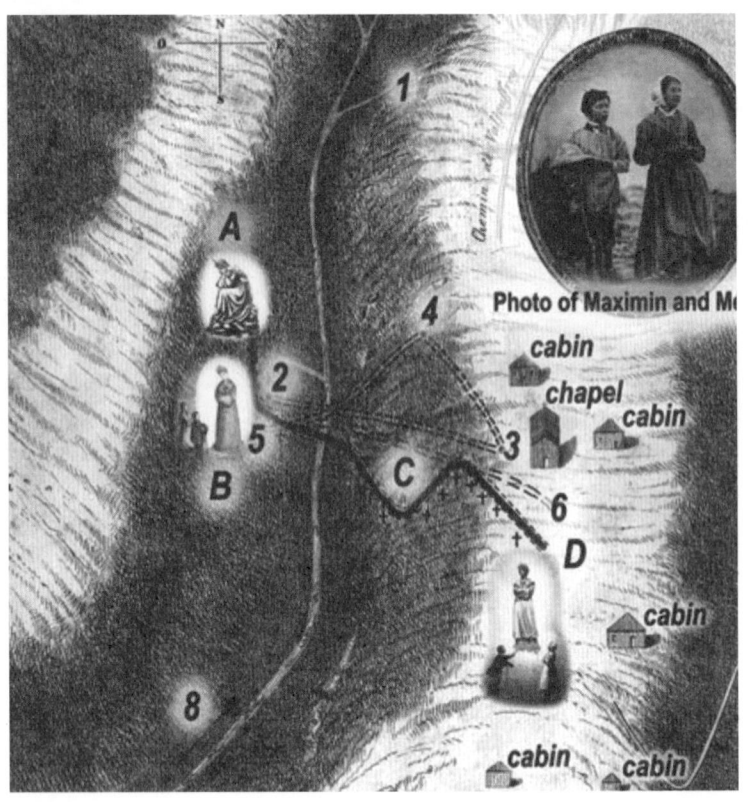

MARY: A: the miraculous fountain where Our Lady was seated, weeping; B: place of their conversation; C: path marked by crosses where Our Lady walked (130 feet); D: the place where Our Lady disappeared.

CHILDREN: 1: the Men's Spring where the children ate; 2: area where they fell asleep; 3: the place where the children looked for their cows; 4: place from where the children saw the globe of light; 5: place of conversation and path the children took to top of knoll (5-6); 6: where children saw Our Lady disappear; 7: the area where the cows were grazing; 8: animals' fountain.

CHAPEL: the provisional chapel;

CABIN: the five cabins built after the Apparition;

NOTE: solid line indicates Our Lady's path; dotted lines indicate the childrens' path.

Part One: Conversion

Chapter One:

La Salette–A Sign of New Times and New Beginnings

Scripture: Luke 2:16-21 (*The visit of the shepherds and the naming of Jesus*)

> *The shepherds went in haste and found Mary and Joseph, and the infant lying in the manger. When they saw this, they made known the message that had been told them about this child. All who heard it were amazed by what had been told them by the shepherds. And Mary kept all these things, reflecting on them in her heart.*
>
> *Then the shepherds returned, glorifying and praising God for all they had heard and seen, just as it had been told to them. When eight days were completed for his circumcision, he was named Jesus, the name given him by the angel before he was conceived in the womb.*

Reflection: Most of us want to look good. Of course, this isn't the world's loftiest motivation but it isn't totally bad either. It's better than not caring at all and better than nothing. It's a beginning. It's a start and, for many of us, a start is already an achievement.

Go ahead and accuse me of being prejudiced, biased, partial and all that, but a good step toward looking good in sober fashion would be to read the message Our Lady gave at La Salette, think about it, then sit yourself down and scribble down some serious resolutions. If you follow even one of them, you will look very, very good – guaranteed.

The beautiful Lady said: *"I have appointed you six days for working. The seventh I have reserved for myself. And no one will give it to me."* If God had obliged everyone to work seven days a week the world would be in an uproar against his harsh demands. Respect for the Lord's day breeds respect for one another. To rest, to visit the sick or the elderly, to eat and talk and play together and pray together as a family makes of Sunday the Lord's day.

Our Lady of La Salette also said: *"The cart drivers cannot swear without bringing in my Son's name."* Respect for the name of Christ means respect for him, and this in turn, is the beginning of respect for one another. Where there is no respect there is no love. To avoid taking the name of Christ as a swear-word is the beginning of a respect that can lead to love of and intimacy with the Lord.

The Lady of La Salette, always weeping as she spoke, went on: *"Do you say your prayers well, my children?"* To pray means to keep in touch with God. Poor communications mean poor relationships. And that goes for our friendship with God also. To pray well, pray simply. If one can't think of anything to say (it happens!) just stay in his presence and say, 'here I am, Lord." He loves your presence before him more than anything else. After all, he died for you, didn't he? You are worth more to him than anything you could say. It is mighty good to think about this, often, this coming year.

She also said in reproach: *"Only a few rather old women go to Mass in the summer."* People "go to Mass only to scoff at religion," she said. Going to Mass every Sunday is a must for coping well with life and its tough problems. This is a perfect resolve to adopt for the coming year.

Our Lady of La Salette continued: *"During Lent they go to the butcher shop like dogs."* Penance is meant to make us generous and able to love deeply. It often takes the form of self-giving to others. There can be no love without penance, self-denial.

These recommendations are really the path to intimacy with the Lord. They also express my love for God, respect for God's name, for Sunday, for the Eucharist are some of the many ways of signifying my love for God and neighbor. Living out any one of these directives will make you feel out of this world – guaranteed.

Reflection Questions:
- When have you made a major change or commitment in your life?

- What major changes for the better have you seen in the life of others?

Prayer:
Mary, Mother of God, your life is a wondrous example of how to follow God's call in our life. As you proclaimed your willingness to be the handmaid of the Lord, you encouraged us to place our lives in God's hands.

Help us appreciate that God is always calling us to begin anew, welcoming new challenges and unexpected possibilities. We can take comfort in the fact that God will walk with us, encouraging us and strengthening us as you did on that Holy Mountain long ago. You encouraged us to live better the basics of our faith, with your example to guide us. May we always place our trust in your loving Son, who lives with the Father and the Holy Spirit, one God, for ever and ever. **Amen.**

La Salette Invocation:
Our Lady of La Salette, Reconciler of Sinners, pray without ceasing for us who have recourse to you.

Chapter Two:

The Man Who Lived the Truth

Scripture: Matthew 11:11-15 (*Jesus' testimony to John*)

Jesus said to the crowds: Amen, I say to you, among those born of women there has been none greater than John the Baptist; yet the least in the kingdom of heaven is greater than he. From the days of John the Baptist until now, the kingdom of heaven suffers violence, and the violent are taking it by force. All the prophets and the law prophesied up to the time of John. And if you are willing to accept it, he is Elijah, the one who is to come. Whoever has ears ought to hear.

Reflection: Prophecy is not easy on the prophet. He or she is possessed by a truth that must be said loud and clear. This truth is unpleasant to most ears and the prophet will probably pay for his prophecy with his life. If he is not killed, he will be thoroughly stripped of all credit and good reputation and finally assassinated by laughter. But true prophets love too much to die. The words they pronounce are not really their own. They are riven with truth and the truth in them will not expire.

We have seen prophets today in the Gandhis, the Berrigans, the Kings, the Sakharovs, the Romeros and that brave man who stood before a tank at Tiananmen Square. No sane person will ever assume the role of prophet. Prophecy is a grace and a terrifying vocation.

John the Baptizer was not only speaking out for a cause. He was announcing a whole new way of relating to God and to life. He was announcing a Person. But now, in these lines, the Person, Jesus, was proclaiming John the Baptist. He was saying, that because he was announcing the Messiah, "history has not known a man born of woman greater than John the Baptist."

There is a new greatness in the land, which is not built on accomplishment or reputation, genius or bloodline. The new greatness consists in belonging to the Kingdom, belonging to the Person of Christ that John the Baptist is announcing. This greatness is the one shared with the Messiah when one belongs to him.

John the Baptist is the new Elijah spoken of in this reading. The person of Elijah has not returned but John plays the role that Elijah played in the Old Testament. He announces the Day of the Lord, when he will come in power, "Now I am sending to you Elijah the prophet, Before the day of the Lord comes, the great and terrible day" (Malachi 3:23).

Who would have suspected that the gentle young woman who became the mother of Jesus at Bethlehem and who remained in obscurity throughout almost the entire New Testament would now inherit the role of prophet. That calling seemed to be natural for her, who loved the people for whom her Son had died.

This time, at La Salette she came to speak to her people about the arm of her Son and urge her people on to conversion. The sweet mother of the classical paintings and the icons could say things such as *"In winter… they go to Mass just to make fun of religion. In Lent they go to the butcher shops like dogs."*

It is part of the prophet's calling to suffer and she did. It is part of the prophet's duty to tell people the unpleasant truths that will change their lives. Prophets speak and they demand to be heard. Reconciliation starts with a person in the middle. At La Salette, it is Mary, the Queen of Prophets.

Reflection Questions:
- When has someone – a family member, a friend, a priest or religious – spoken words that changed you or others in some way?

- When have you been called to speak challenging words to others – your children or acquaintances?

Prayer:
Mary, Queen of Prophets, you can stand proudly in the family of prophetic witnesses who spoke difficult words – all for the sake of love. You reminded us of the importance of celebrating the Eucharist regularly, and using other Lenten habits of faith in our attempt to follow your Son each day.

May your words sink deep into our minds and hearts and help us to become better witnesses of your Son. Through your powerful intercession, may we become reconcilers to all those whom we meet along the way. We ask this through your loving Son, who lives with the Father and the Holy Spirit, one God, for ever and ever. **Amen**.

Invocation:
Our Lady of La Salette, Reconciler of Sinners, pray without ceasing for us who have recourse to you.

Chapter Three:

What Faith in God Means

Scripture: John 10:31-42 (*Incident on the Feast of the Dedication in Jerusalem*)

When the Jews again picked up rocks to stone him, Jesus answered them, "I have shown you many good works from my Father. For which of these are you trying to stone me?" The Jews answered him, "We are not stoning you for a good work but for blasphemy. You, a man, are making yourself God."

Jesus answered them, "Is it not written in your law, 'I said, "You are gods"'? If it calls them gods to whom the word of God came, and scripture cannot be set aside, can you say that the one whom the Father has consecrated and sent into the world blasphemes because I said, 'I am the Son of God'? If I do not perform my Father's works, do not believe me; but if I perform them, even if you do not believe me, believe the works, so that you may realize [and understand] that the Father is in me and I am in the Father." [Then] they tried again to arrest him; but he escaped from their power.

He went back across the Jordan to the place where John first baptized, and there he remained. Many came to him and said, "John performed no sign, but everything John said about this man was true." And many there began to believe in him.

Reflection: The Jews in all their history had never seen the likes of this man who proclaimed himself Son of God. Of course, everyone is a son or daughter of God. But this man said that God was his real Father. At the close of his speech, following the parable of the Good Shepherd, Christ stated that not one of these sheep of his would be "snatched out" of his hand because no one can snatch the sheep out of the Father's hand. Then Christ scraped every single nerve ending in his audience when he said, "The Father and I are one" (John 10:30). Hence, the reason for the sheep's safety is that both the Father and Christ, being one, agree never to abandon the sheep.

Legally Christ was within his rights; the law condemned only an outright declaration of divinity by someone who pronounced the name of God while doing so. But all knew the meaning of Christ's words. The spirit of the law angered the Jews beyond the point of verbal condemnation. The time for talk had ceased. "…the Jews again picked up rocks to stone him."

We don't associate stones with faith. As they had done before (see John 8:59), the Jews intended to stone him. It is easy here to summon up empathy for Christ and denigration for the Jews. Once again we are faced with the basic problem of faith in John: we are not urged to believe in God's power and majesty, his dominion over all things and his sovereign creative strength; these are implied but not immediately brought to the fore. What we are called upon to believe is the depth of God's affection. If power and majesty and creative sovereignty are understood in all this, so be it. But the basic plea is for openness to a faith made possible only by the quickening presence of God.

The reading illustrates the power of this kind of affection, which seeks to draw to itself both friend and foe. All that God does is done out of love. When Christ said, "The Father and I are one" (John 10:30), he meant it not as an inflammatory statement but a loving one, even in view of the Jews' murderous intent.

Jesus' admirable works are to be sought not only in the changing of water into wine, in the saving of the royal official's son from death, in the healing of the paralytic at Bethesda, in the feeding of five thousand from a few loaves and fish or in the taming of the storm on the lake. For Christ, self-revelation as God proved to be a lethal undertaking, and necessitated as much fondness for, and attachment to people than the most astounding miraculous feat.

A rain of stone missiles coming at you is just not worth the sermon, unless you mean what you say and love the stone-thrower enough to say it. There is no miracle in this because a miracle could never describe and encompass such a thing. But there is an eternal passion for people, one that soars beyond the wonders of creation itself and can only be measured by the heart of a living God.

There is a passing mention of John the Baptist, as if the writer intended to close some huge parenthesis. John's message had been the revelation of Christ to the world. "Behold, the Lamb of God" (John 1:29), he had said. His first designation is that of witness (John 1:6). His work is now accomplished. To reveal the Son, to reveal God had been his mission. Christ now fulfills this calling. But both will die carrying out this mission.

Without cynicism one can say that caring for people brings its share of pain – joys too, of course, but pain in abundance. It is pain born of love, though, and that washes out the cynicism. *"How long a time have I suffered for you!"* said the Lady at La Salette. *"You will never be able to recompense the pains I have taken for you"*, she said again. We might be tempted to look at the *"good things"* from heaven, like stones that become mounds of wheat and self-sown potatoes as shining examples of God's tender loving care for us. However there are also the sufferings, and the thoughtlessness – *"You paid no heed!"* – and the flow of tears that flood the heart and cannot be held back.

There is cause for peace in all this, even for the most distraught person. There is hope, too. The warnings and threats of La Salette contain as much affection as the promises and the caring, thoughtful, story of the farm of Coin.

Reflection Questions:
• What event (in your life or that of others) has God performed that strengthened your faith?

• When, in your interaction with another, have you perhaps seemed to be angry when your true motivation was your love of that person? Did they – at that time or later – understand (or not) your loving concern for them?

Prayer:
Our Lady of Compassion, your loving concern for your people was more than obvious in your visit at La Salette. Your concern for your people's at times heedless response came from your passionate desire to help your children by inviting them to deeper faith in your Son.

Your words about conversion were not a threat but a compassionate invitation to follow the path your Son gave us. May our belief and trust in your Son blossom through your intercession. We ask this through your loving Son, who lives with the Father and the Holy Spirit, one God, for ever and ever. **Amen.**

Invocation:
Our Lady of La Salette, Reconciler of Sinners, pray without ceasing for us who have recourse to you.

Chapter Four:

When Concern is Hard to Kill

Scripture: Matthew 21:33-43,45-46 (*The parable of the tenants*)

Jesus said to the chief priests and elders of the people: "Hear another parable. There was a landowner who planted a vineyard, put a hedge around it, dug a wine press in it, and built a tower. Then he leased it to tenants and went on a journey.

When vintage time drew near, he sent his servants to the tenants to obtain his produce. But the tenants seized the servants and one they beat, another they killed, and a third they stoned. Again he sent other servants, more numerous than the first ones, but they treated them in the same way.

Finally, he sent his son to them, thinking, 'They will respect my son.' But when the tenants saw the son, they said to one another, 'This is the heir. Come, let us kill him and acquire his inheritance.' They seized him, threw him out of the vineyard, and killed him.

What will the owner of the vineyard do to those tenants when he comes?" They answered him, "He will put those wretched men to a wretched death and lease his vineyard to other tenants who will give him the produce at the proper times."

Jesus said to them, "Did you never read in the scriptures: 'The stone that the builders rejected has become the cornerstone; by the Lord has this been done, and it is wonderful in our eyes'? Therefore, I say to you, the kingdom of God will be taken away from you and given to a people that will produce its fruit.

When the chief priests and the Pharisees heard his parables, they knew that he was speaking about them. And although they were attempting to arrest him, they feared the crowds, for they regarded him as a prophet.

Reflection: Some lovers send greeting cards. Some write poems or letters. Some extravagant people may resort to skywriting. Nowadays, email and other electronic methods have come into the picture. And of course, there is always the cellphone.

If human love only wanly reflects the love of the Almighty, one wonders how God expresses love for those that came right out of the divine hand. Of course, there is the simple fact of our own existence, creation all around us with blessings that are beyond even the most sophisticated computer. In its simple, direct manner, the gospel becomes a most wondrous love message. Elizabeth Barrett Browning wrote to Robert, "How do I love you? Let me count the ways…"

In this rather violent gospel reading, the Lord is the wealthy landowner who loves his vineyard. The vineyard of the gospel is the people of God. The various methods and techniques of vineyard cultivation taken by the owner, tell of his love for it. "There was a landowner who planted a vineyard, put a hedge around it, dug a wine press in it, and built a tower." Not the least sign – mysterious as it may be – of love is God's initiative in creating the vine, fashioning a people in order to love it and care for it. This prompts us to remember that existence – even if we have it preceded by "mere" – is still the most basic and original of all personal blessings.

Concern for the vineyard is one of the salient features of this parable (note the watchtower). Another is the broad trust God has in people when the landowner entrusts the vineyard to tenants and gives them responsibility for it. The landowner's trust is not only verbal. He has enough faith in the tenants to leave and go to "another country."

The landowner, who is God, is not through with concern for his vineyard. The parable expresses God's deep interest in people. With time, the landowner dispatches servants to collect the produce of his land but the tenants seized his slaves and beat one, killed another, and stoned another. The landowner sent a second delegation and the tenants treated it the same way. The master of the vineyard sent his own son to them, saying, "They will respect my son." But they "seized him, threw him out of the vineyard, and killed him."

The parable makes a single point starkly clear: the Landowner Lord pursues his people relentlessly. There are no great declarations of love in this passage. Three times – the Hebrew's perfect number – the Landowner sends his prophets to save the vineyard. Three times readers are treated to violence that reminds us of our own contemporary savagery. This is love in the face of more than passing rejection. This is loving pursuit in the presence of violence and death.

Every season is a season of conversion and change. The Lord has called us more than three times. We may not have killed prophets or his Son but we may have induced the gift of living faith into a long and deep coma. The danger is not so much that the Lord will cease calling but that we may no longer be able to hear his voice.

The apparition of La Salette is itself a call. The extraordinary means God takes to attract our attention, the importance of the person God sends manifests the importance of the call and the urgency of the message. The apparition and the message breathe concern.

The visual nature of the phenomenon – the striking dress, the tears, the blinding light – all stir the memory. The words are vehement, at times threatening. The call is clearly for conversion. La Salette gives us the sharp message that someone cares enough to call and call again. To speak. To upbraid. To weep.

As she left the children, she said to them, *"Well, my children, you will make this known to all my people."* Deeply felt concern always makes sure the word is given, the message is heard. Again, before disappearing from their view, she repeated to Maximin and Melanie, *"Well, my children, you will make this known to all my people."* In this case, repetition is an expression of concern.

Reflection Questions:
- When did you powerfully notice another's true love for you by what they said or did for you?
- When have you experienced a "season of change" in your life?

Prayer:
Mary, Concerned Mother of Us All, in your visit at La Salette you expressed your overwhelming concern for your wayward people. Your initial prophetic words got our attention but your gentle interest in Maximin and his father in his experience at the field of Coin was a powerful example of your (and God's) concern for the challenges of life that can easily overwhelm us.

Through your intercession, help us to believe and trust more strongly in your Son's concern for us, his people. And may we, in turn, assist others who, without our help, may lose hope amid the challenges of this life. We ask this through your loving Son, who lives with the Father and the Holy Spirit, one God, for ever and ever. **Amen**.

Invocation:
Our Lady of La Salette, Reconciler of Sinners, pray without ceasing for us who have recourse to you.

Chapter Five:

A Question of Authority

Scripture: Matthew 21:23-27 (*The authority of Jesus is questioned*)

When (Jesus) had come into the temple area, the chief priests and the elders of the people approached him as he was teaching and said, "By what authority are you doing these things? And who gave you this authority?"

Jesus said to them in reply, "I shall ask you one question, and if you answer it for me, then I shall tell you by what authority I do these things. Where was John's baptism from? Was it of heavenly or of human origin?" They discussed this among themselves and said, "If we say 'Of heavenly origin,' he will say to us, 'Then why did you not believe him?' But if we say, 'Of human origin,' we fear the crowd, for they all regard John as a prophet." So they said to Jesus in reply, "We do not know." He himself said to them, "Neither shall I tell you by what authority I do these things."

Reflection: This is not the New Testament's most quoted passage. It is a discussion between Jesus and Jewish authorities and discussions, especially discussions on abstract topics, do not make for page-turning copy. Jesus had evicted the money changers from the temple and, understandably, the Jewish rabbis wanted to know by what authority he could do this, by what authority he could teach the doctrine of God.

Rabbinical discussions were often conducted not in question-and-answer form, but in question-and-question style. In reply to a question came another question. The Jews asked Jesus, "Where was John's baptism from? Was it of heavenly or of human origin?"

Jesus answers with a question of his own, "I shall ask you one question... Did the baptism of John come from heaven, or was it of human origin?" They conferred with one another on this and saw that if they admitted John's baptism as coming from heaven then Jesus would ask them why they didn't believe in John's baptism.

If they said that John's baptism was from earth they risked the anger of the crowds who had John the Baptist in high regard. "So they said to Jesus in reply, "We do not know." He himself said to them, "Neither shall I tell you by what authority I do these things." As John P. Meier writes in his book, *The Vision of Matthew*, "The leaders cannot say because of ignorance; Jesus chooses not to say, because his teaching authority is superior to these incompetents."

Jesus did not claim authority on his own. There was no question here of authority acquired on the basis of personality, knowledge, intelligence or quality of character. The problem was origin: where did Christ get his authority to speak and teach as he did? Who gave him this authority?

Matthew is not only writing for distant posterity but also for his own church whose members were locked in a struggle over authority with the Jews of their time and place. This declaration from Matthew in the words of Christ must have come to them as a welcome buttress and affirmation.

In the end, it is a question of confidence. Authority gives credence to what a person says and does. For us who read Matthew today, Christ's authority strengthens our faith in Christ's sayings on the Kingdom, his Father, on charity and mutual respect and love and especially on God's constant and gracious love for everyone.

At La Salette, Our Lady spoke in the name of her Son. She clearly did not say what she said on her own authority. She reminds people of the Mass, the day, Sunday, reserved for the Lord, penance, prayer and respect and honor for the Name of her Son. These are all God-centered commandments and the Lady speaks about them on the authority of her Son. She mentions this "Son" repeatedly throughout the apparition, so that there is no doubt about the origin of her message.

She spoke in his name and she sent two children, two unlikely messengers with an authority of their own to speak what she had spoken as she herself had received from her Son the authority to speak of the Word.

At the close of Matthew's gospel, Christ said: "All power in heaven and on earth has been given to me. Go, therefore, and make disciples of all nations..." (Matthew 28:18b-19a). At La Salette, Mary's farewell to Maximin and Melanie has a similar ring: *"Well, my children, you will make this known to all my people."*

Of course, the second, Mary's mandate, does not have the authority of the first in the gospel of Matthew but both are inspired by one love lavished on the whole world.

Reflection Questions:
- Why does the Lord invite you in the scriptures and in the La Salette message to celebrate the Eucharist regularly?

- When have you encouraged others to keep their faith alive by becoming active believers?

Prayer:
Virgin Most Powerful, your surprising visit at La Salette to the two unassuming children, was a pure gift for God. Your stature as God's representative was not initially appreciated by the two children. Only afterwards, others surmised your true identity as Mother of us all. Others also noticed that your weeping expressed

in obvious ways your deep love for your Son and for your needy people.

We can easily see the reflection of your Son in your words and loving attitude during your brief visit on that mountaintop. May we always give thanks to God for such a special, intimate gift. We ask this through your loving Son, who lives with the Father and the Holy Spirit, one God, for ever and ever. **Amen**.

Invocation:
Our Lady of La Salette, Reconciler of Sinners, pray without ceasing for us who have recourse to you.

Chapter Six:

There is Always a Reason Not to Dance

Scripture: Matthew 11:16-19 (*The parable of the children*)

Jesus said to the crowds: "To what shall I compare this generation? It is like children who sit in marketplaces and call to one another, 'We played the flute for you, but you did not dance, we sang a dirge but you did not mourn.' For John came neither eating nor drinking, and they said, 'He is possessed by a demon.' The Son of Man came eating and drinking and they said, 'Look, he is a glutton and a drunkard, a friend of tax collectors and sinners.' But wisdom is vindicated by her works."

Reflection: It has happened to everyone over the age of ten, that some days you just cannot win, you just cannot make people understand what you are trying to do. If you fast, you are ruining your health. If you relax a while, you are a hedonist, if you go on a trip, you can't stay in place, if you work long hours you are compulsive, if you don't work while people are looking, you are lazy.

John the Baptist came wearing cutting-edge desert garb and eating grasshoppers, preaching and baptizing with ascetic zeal and they said, "He is possessed by a demon." Christ came eating and drinking with saint and sinner alike and people said, "Look, a glutton and a drunkard, a friend of tax collectors and sinners!"

Who are "they"? Matthew places them together and calls them generically "this generation". These are the people, the crowds who refuse to believe in Jesus, to have a hospitable mind, or who foster a closed mind and unwelcoming spirit.

Real life experience teaches us that very often the acceptance of Christ in faith hinges on practical life matters and vested interests. Certain habits and privileges, certain modes of conduct, personal beliefs, prejudices and convictions can effectively diminish the freedom we need to accept and embrace the following of Christ in faith. Even once faith has been accepted, these obstacles prevent people from progressing further in knowledge of the Lord and intimacy with him.

Following Christ – shaping behavior in accordance with the convictions of faith – demands a sense of adventure and a willingness to change. This latter – a willingness to change – is often the deciding factor. The coming of Christ in the world and in our individual lives calls for myriad changes, some uncomfortable.

Conversion is change. Reconciliation is change. Renewal is change. All of these presuppose certain dispositions in people. They demand the nerves of the sky diver who leaps from the plane and that same sky diver's faith in the opening of the parachute. It would seem that even for the sick and bed-ridden Christian, a sense of adventure and a willingness to constantly turn toward the Lord are requisites for discipleship.

The Lord, born in a stable, may be the Prince of Peace but he has come to bring fire onto the earth. Eating and drinking may be pleasant tasks, but eating and drinking with sinners and tax collectors meant trouble, the very opposite of peace. Healing on the Sabbath, conversing with Samaritans and women in public places, these are not capricious acts meant for exhibition and show. These are signs of an inward belief in a God of truth, whose motives are love and the welfare of people.

It is part of the absurdities of our lives that performing a good act is very often harrowingly difficult while indulgence and going with the crowd can be accomplished with downhill ease.

One thing is clear from today's gospel: the present-day Christ is still the Gospel Lord. That has not changed. He is still a sign of contradiction. He will still create storms and upset for the sake of peace. He still speaks out the unpleasant truth and he still can cause trouble for the sake of justice.

John and Jesus had varying approaches to service and people but they had a common characteristic: they both loved the crowds who came to them and, for that reason, hated compromise.

The Lady's tears at La Salette should not be mistaken for weakness. *"I will be forced to let go the arm of my Son."* The reproaches come without hesitation: blasphemy; dishonoring the Lord's day; going to the butcher shop like dogs; the threat of famine, death, of rotting wheat and potatoes. One senses that these words are issued fourth straight from love. There is no compromise here because loving and serving a Friend allows for no compromises. The message of La Salette may have been tough on us. It was tougher on her.

Reflection Questions:
- What person do you know who has an open, welcoming spirit?
- Have anyone's tears affected you deeply?

Prayer:
Tearful Mother of La Salette, your visit with us shows your love of your Son and your deep concern for us, your wayward people. Your tears continue to touch our heart and open our minds to your words and witness.

We promise to heed your tearful pleas and open our hearts to the transforming words you utter with unimaginable compassion and caring. In turn you ask us to reach out in faith and make your message known especially to those who have lost their way. We ask this through your intercession and through the grace of loving Son, who lives with the Father and the Holy Spirit, one God, for ever and ever. **Amen**.

Invocation:
Our Lady of La Salette, Reconciler of Sinners, pray without ceasing for us who have recourse to you.

Part Two:
Called to Do God's Will

Chapter Seven:

Proceeding in Haste

Scripture: Luke 1:39-45 (*Mary visits Elizabeth*)

Mary set out in those days and traveled to the hill country in haste to a town of Judah, where she entered the house of Zechariah and greeted Elizabeth. When Elizabeth heard Mary's greeting, the infant leaped in her womb, and Elizabeth, filled with the Holy Spirit, cried out in a loud voice and said, "Most blessed are you among women, and blessed is the fruit of your womb. And how does this happen to me, that the mother of my Lord should come to me? For at the moment the sound of your greeting reached my ears, the infant in my womb leaped for joy. Blessed are you who believed that what was spoken to you by the Lord would be fulfilled."

Reflection: The author of the gospel of Luke has a unique way of showing us the soul of the Virgin Mary. He does not say that she is a true disciple; that she loves the Lord deeply; that she has a strong prayer life; that she is eager to live out in daily life what she is contemplating in her heart; that her spiritual life is not centered on her own existence but extends outward to the people she knows and loves.

Her love for God is not the kind that manifests itself only in words, but the words she does pronounce become a charter and a way of life. When the angel told her he was from God and that this Lord wanted to become human through her, she sought to clear her own conscience with one question before she readily and decisively said, "Behold, I am the handmaid of the Lord. May it be done to me according to your word" (Luke 1:38).

The gospel gives the clear impression that Mary left quickly to see her pregnant cousin Elizabeth. As soon as the angel left her, the gospel narrative remains taut as the author continues, "During those days Mary set out and traveled to the hill country in haste to a town of Judah, where she entered the house of Zechariah and greeted Elizabeth" (Luke 1:39-40).

Devotion to God goes in tandem with devotion and fidelity to people. And she went in haste. Her destination was not a walk but a journey, about 80 to 100 miles distant from Nazareth. The angel had told her about Elizabeth's pregnancy; there was no command to visit her. But the mere implication was an order and she set out without delay.

Admirably, in a few lines, the author of the gospel gives us a simple but eloquent description of Mary. The "yes" she gave to the Lord at the Annunciation was not the generosity that gave something away. It was the greatness of soul that gave herself away as gift. This was the "yes" of a lifetime. God was not asking her to give *a moment of her life* but to *give her life in a moment*. It would seem, upon reflection, that when God comes into a life, God changes it forever. To this day, Mary's role as Mother of the Church, as intercessor, stems from that first and everlasting "yes" she gave at Nazareth over 2,000 years ago.

Clearly, La Salette reveals more than a message of words. The Lady is accomplishing an ongoing "ministry" of her own from heaven. La Salette shows only a brief moment of that work. Reconcilers don't have it easy. *"How long a time I have suffered for you! If I want my Son not to abandon you, I am obliged to plead with him constantly... However much you do, you will never be able to recompense the pains I have taken for you."*

The two children, Maximin and Melanie, accepted to relay the message to "all my people" as the Lady said. But then, their lives too were forever transformed. That mission took them away from their beloved mountains and their simple lives. They accomplished the mission the Lady had confided to them but the task was a crushing one.

At the end of his life, Maximin regretted the uprooted existence he had to live as one of the famous children of La Salette. God had demanded much from Maximin and Melanie and they had given it. What God had demanded was a lifetime of trial and suffering. In the end, they could look back with the satisfaction and the gratitude that come from having accepted to be witnesses and never having betrayed their trust.

They had given their own "yes" and they had become the first Missionaries of La Salette.

Reflection Questions:
- How have you been inspired by Mary's words and example at La Salette?

- How have you (or another) been helped in time of need?

Prayer:
Mary, Mother of God's People, your response to those in need was all-embracing. Your visit to Elizabeth was prompted from your own appreciation of what it means to bear new life within you and its instant responsibilities.

Your selfless response in helping another is a wondrous reminder that we are called to be responsive to the needs of others, not counting the cost. Support us in responding fully to your mandate to proclaim your message, and help us to be persistent in inviting and encouraging others to follow your Son. We ask this through your intercession and through the grace of your loving Son, who lives with the Father and the Holy Spirit, one God, for ever and ever. **Amen.**

Invocation:
Our Lady of La Salette, Reconciler of Sinners, pray without ceasing for us who have recourse to you.

Chapter Eight:

Blessed Be the Lord

Scripture: Luke 1: 67-79 (*The Canticle of Zechariah*)

Zechariah his father, filled with the Holy Spirit, prophesied, saying: "Blessed be the Lord, the God of Israel; for he has come to his people and set them free. He has raised up for us a mighty Savior, born of the house of his servant David. Through his prophets he promised of old that he would save us from our enemies, from the hands of all who hate us. He promised to show mercy to our fathers and to remember his holy covenant. This was the oath he swore to our father Abraham: to set us free from the hand of our enemies, free to worship him without fear, holy and righteous in his sight all the days of our life.

You, my child, shall be called the prophet of the Most High, for you will go before the Lord to prepare his way, to give his people knowledge of salvation by the forgiveness of their sins. In the tender compassion of our God the dawn from on high shall break upon us, to shine on those who dwell in darkness and the shadow of death, and to guide our feet into the way of peace."

Reflection: Luke is the gospel of songs. Here, we find the song called the Benedictus. Luke also contains the biblical half of the *Hail Mary*, the virgin's *Magnificat* as well as the elderly Simeon's song of confidence in the Lord, known as the *Nunc Dimittis*. Zechariah was happy with a happiness that made him sing the praises of God. He was "filled with the Holy Spirit" as Elizabeth was earlier when she addressed Mary and said, "Blessed are you among women, and blessed is the fruit of your womb" (Luke 1:41-42). When one is filled with the Holy Spirit, one blesses the Lord. Praise and blessing are a sign of the Spirit.

Zechariah blesses God for visiting. To visit here means to call upon people, to become aware of them, to be present to them – all quite elementary and exactly because of that, vital. The intent of this verse is not only to say that God knows we exist but that God knows us well.

This will not be a formal visit, one based on manners and deference. God's visits are always hands-on calls; they accomplish something: God redeems people, sets them free, unshackles them. This is salvation and it remains our most valid reason for praising and thanking. Zechariah praises God who alone came to save. God came in person and accomplished this freeing act "in the flesh". This is mysterious and the *Benedictus*, like all great songs, holds a mystery in its air.

Zechariah had other reasons for giving praise. He blessed Yahweh for being faithful throughout the centuries in spite of the people's infidelities. God remembered all the covenants made with Israel as well as "the oath that he swore to our ancestor Abraham, to set us free... free to worship him without fear...." This is the oath God swore after having spared Isaac from the sacrificing knife of Abraham: "...because you acted as you did in not withholding from me your son, your only one, I will bless you..." (Genesis 22:16b-17a).

If the gospels have one overriding purpose, it is to recall the continuity of the traditions and prophecies of old with the realities of the "new way." Zechariah's hymn sings of salvation wrought by God, and if there is one truth that can be assumed it is that God can be trusted, believed and believed in. God would not be God without it.

Perhaps the last word of this song is the one that the world of this year would most prize: peace. Zechariah is indeed a prophet since a prophet's voice praises as well as predicts. He sings that this peace is one that we can receive from God if we walk in his ways: "to guide our feet into the way of peace."

Peace is a gift but it is possible to be unable to receive it, to have a heart and a soul that are completely incompatible with God's peace. This peace is more than the absence of strife but a combination of order, joy, trust, the knowledge of being saved and salvation itself. The peace hailed here has an eloquent echo at the close of the gospel, when Jesus greeted the disciples of Emmaus: "Peace be with you," he said to them (see *the New Jerome Biblical Commentary*, Luke 1:79 and 24:36).

Mary's apparition at La Salette is a call to praise and bless the Lord. She reminds people to observe the day that the Lord has reserved for worship. She says that *"those who drive carts cannot swear without throwing in my Son's name. These are the two things that make the arm of my Son so heavy"*, she concludes. It is one thing to be visited by God and quite another to accept the visit in welcome.

A good candidate for the ultimate sin would be ignoring God to the point of disrespect. A mind and soul thus inhabited are unable to accept the gift of peace. When Zechariah sang of God visiting his people, he sang of God's regard for them, of God's "taking note" of them and "minding" them.

At La Salette, Mary twice reproaches her people for paying *"no heed"*. There is no insult equal to that of being ignored. It is the sin of doing nothing, the ultimate affront to One who insists on visiting his people.

Reflection Questions:
• When have you or others been called to become reconcilers (or peacemakers) in personal or family disputes or other challenging situations?

- When have you actively invited or encouraged another to become active in their faith?

Prayer:
Mary, Faithful Mother of La Salette, your words at La Salette were truly a dialogue, asking a response from the two children and from us. You list how we have not been responsive to your Son's will in our lives and need to reform our lives.

Continue to remind us to pray each day, treasure the Eucharist, respect your Son's name, and become active in other habits which can strengthen our faith. We ask this through your intercession and through the grace of loving Son, who lives with the Father and the Holy Spirit, one God, for ever and ever. **Amen.**

Invocation:
Our Lady of La Salette, Reconciler of Sinners, pray without ceasing for us who have recourse to you.

Chapter Nine:

To the Childlike

Scripture: Luke 10:21-24 (*Praise of the Father and the privileges of discipleship*)

Jesus rejoiced in the Holy Spirit and said, "I give you praise, Father, Lord of heaven and earth, for although you have hidden these things from the wise and the learned you have revealed them to the childlike. Yes, Father, such has been your gracious will. All things have been handed over to me by my Father. No one knows who the Son is except the Father, and who the Father is except the Son and anyone to whom the Son wishes to reveal him."

Turning to the disciples in private he said, "Blessed are the eyes that see what you see. For I say to you, many prophets and kings desired to see what you see, but did not see it, and to hear what you hear, but did not hear it."

Reflection: The Christ of the gospels is a happy person. There are times when his happiness surges out of him and erupts into glorious joy, like in this passage. Why does he rejoice? Because, lo and behold, God's friendship is not reserved to smart people and adults. The Father of Christ is the Father of little children. He calls them "the childlike". He adds that the Father has graciously willed it so. The will of God is that children and all who resemble them in spirit should enter into God's love and friendship.

Children don't fit in the kingdom of God because they are innocent and without sin, because they are morally intact. They are prized and become the cause of Christ's joy because they are unassuming, candid and not too proud to depend on other people. The disciples and those who resemble them struggle for a toehold on prestige, always planning for place and power and who will take the seats at his right or left. Children don't care where they sit. Simplicity is to faith as wing is to flight.

People spend lifetimes searching for Wisdom and there is a cache of it here. Knowledge of God comes not with depth of learning and brocade sophistication nor is it the heritage of the obsessively simplistic. On the contrary, knowledge of Christ comes with simplicity of heart.

Why does Christ rejoice in all this? He has just seen his disciples return from a preaching mission. He sees their openness and their joy at having spread the good news of Christ. Why again is Christ so utterly joyful in the Spirit? Because perhaps, he sees that no container can contain an ocean but a human heart can hold the Divine. This is something to rejoice in.

Many who have known La Salette have wondered why the Lady chose Maximin and Melanie for her witnesses. Since she had such a choice of seers, why on earth choose Maximin and Melanie? Then we realize that this is the same Lady who once sang, "He has thrown down the rulers from their thrones but lifted up the lowly" (Luke 1:52). We are always too eager to call them simple-minded. They were also simple-hearted and the Lady spoke to their hearts as well as to their minds. The choice of these two children remains one of La Salette's most significant teachings.

If we needed to know who are God's favorites on this planet, we could benefit by looking at La Salette.

Reflection Questions:
- Whom do you know (or know about) who has a "childlike" faith?

- How can Mary's choice of Maximin and Melanie give hope to ordinary people like you?

Prayer:
Mary, Lover of All God's Children, we truly appreciate the fact that God has hidden things from the wise and the learned and revealed them to the merest children. That was again seen in Mary's choice of these two poor, unknown and uneducated children.

In God's ways, the simplicity of heart of these two children attracted Mary, confounded some experts and enlightened the truly learned. By your intercession, continue to enlighten our faith through the grace of your loving Son, who lives with the Father and the Holy Spirit, one God, for ever and ever. **Amen**.

Invocation:
Our Lady of La Salette, Reconciler of Sinners, pray without ceasing for us who have recourse to you.

Chapter Ten:

That Big, Strong Gospel Keystone

Scripture: Matthew 7:21,24-27 (*The true disciple and the two foundations*)

> *Jesus said to his disciples: "Not everyone who says to me, 'Lord, Lord,' will enter the Kingdom of heaven, but only the one who does the will of my Father in heaven. "Everyone who listens to these words of mine and acts on them will be like a wise man who built his house on rock. The rain fell, the floods came, and the winds blew and buffeted the house. But it did not collapse; it had been set solidly on rock. And everyone who listens to these words of mine but does not act on them will be like a fool who built his house on sand. The rain fell, the floods came, and the winds blew and buffeted the house. And it collapsed and was completely ruined."*

Reflection: There are still many people who try to get down to the bedrock-basics of life. We say that life is too short to waste on second rate issues. As the years progress, we wonder if we have squandered too many hours and days poking at life instead of living it. This gospel reading has much to say about this, and the passage is not one of those soaring speeches and often-quoted verses that are the stuff of sanctuary banners. You will not often find the "will of God" on posters or in retreat slogans.

And yet it should be up there on church steeples with the cross and all the artwork. Nothing in the gospels and indeed, in all of world literature, proves the worth of love more than the oneness of it. To do the will of the beloved is love's heaviest burden and most delightful challenge. We sing of love's manifold unions but none has a firmer grasp and a warmer clasp than "wasting" one's strength and committing one's life to the velvet task of pleasing the other.

This type of union with God is expressed in the gospel as entering the Kingdom. The Kingdom of God is God's life and heart. The "only" person who will enter that heart and that kingdom is the one who seeks and finds ways of pleasing the Beloved. Doing God's will, by the way, cannot improve God's lot or fortune, and so, doing God's will means what St. Irenaeus defined it to be back in the second century: "God's will is humanity fully alive." This is the pithiest description ever written of the will of God.

In this world of meetings, retreats, seminars, encounters and conventions about priorities, this priority has the highest rating. It helps to understand the importance of this will of God to note that this passage forms part of the Sermon on the Mount. It is Christ's first of five great sermons in Matthew and is in itself a compendium of the entire gospel.

People on every continent have been seeking wisdom since the beginning of time. Here Christ says that "Everyone who listens to these words of mine and acts on them will be like a wise man who built his house on rock." There probably is no more comforting word in the world for us buffeted, beaten and weeping humans than this blanket guarantee of soul-strength and wisdom. The rains come and the winds blow strong enough to roil the oceans but this man's house stands because it has been "set solidly on rock."

When the beautiful Lady appeared at La Salette, she invited the children to come closer to her: *"Come near, my children, don't be afraid. I am here to tell you great news."*

The great news she had in mind contained many different items but she had one overriding concern to share with the children: "*If my people will not submit, I will be forced to let go the arm of my Son. It is so strong and so heavy, that I can no longer hold it back.*" The mother of the Lord comes directly to the bedrock of our religion and our existence.

Her first sentence deals with obedience and submission, admittedly no Gallup poll popularity winners in our day. That first declaration encompasses the entire discourse. Indeed, the discourse only itemizes this first statement. We see the will of God mentioned in the Lord's first sermon of his ministry and we see the very same idea in first place in the Beautiful Lady's discourse. Surely, they've been talking to each other.

The gospel is Revelation and the discourse does not oblige anyone to believe in it for salvation. But since the Lady was sent to pronounce it, it would be rash not to heed it. For those of us who seek soul tranquility and serenity of heart, doing the will of God – doing "God's thing", as it were – is a prime must. For fullness of life and for fulfillment of the heart, both the gospel and the discourse are on a parallel course. The Lady came to remind us that our happiness and joy were still on God's mind.

Reflection Questions:
- In what important situation in your life did you feel that you were doing what God wanted you to do?

- What faith-practices do you do to strengthen your faith on the rock that is Jesus?

Prayer:
Mary, Mother of Wisdom, we, your children, wish to sit at the fount of your wisdom and hear the words of your Son echo for us in your loving presence on the Holy Mountain of La Salette.

As you consecrated yourself to the will of God at your Annunciation, so we too wish to follow the will of God by taking concrete steps to make your message known. May your attitude of humble service and your example of total dedication to your Son and his Kingdom be for us the center of our lives. We ask this through your intercession and through the grace of loving Son, who lives with the Father and the Holy Spirit, one God, for ever and ever. **Amen**.

Invocation:
Our Lady of La Salette, Reconciler of Sinners, pray without ceasing for us who have recourse to you.

Part Three:
The Generosity of the Cross

Chapter Eleven:

Repaid in Secret

Reflection: Matthew 6:1-6,16-18 (*Teaching about almsgiving, prayer and fasting*)

Jesus said to his disciples: "Take care not to perform righteous deeds in order that people may see them; otherwise, you will have no recompense from your heavenly Father.

When you give alms, do not blow a trumpet before you, as the hypocrites do in the synagogues and in the streets to win the praise of others. Amen, I say to you, they have received their reward. But when you give alms, do not let your left hand know what your right is doing, so that your almsgiving may be secret. And your Father who sees in secret will repay you.

"When you pray, do not be like the hypocrites, who love to stand and pray in the synagogues and on street corners so that others may see them. Amen, I say to you, they have received their reward. But when you pray, go to your inner room, close the door, and pray to your Father in secret. And your Father who sees in secret will repay you.

"When you fast, do not look gloomy like the hypocrites. They neglect their appearance, so that they may appear to others to be fasting. Amen, I say to you, they have received their reward. But when you fast, anoint your head and wash your face, so

that you may not appear to others to be fasting, except to your Father who is hidden. And your Father who sees what is hidden will repay you.

Reflection: Many biblical words quickly center in on crucial and meaningful ideas. Almsgiving, prayer and fasting were very important words in Judaism and those who practiced them were said to walk in holiness. One thing is clear: these works are not an end in themselves but a means to worship and glorify God. With a little discretion, almsgiving, prayer and fasting can be done in secrecy, away from notice and stares. But they can also "discreetly" be accomplished for all to see. Then, the praise and glory reserved for God alone would come raining down on the individual and the whole effort comes to ruin.

"When you give alms, do not let your left hand know what your right is doing." This does not mean that almsgiving has to be impersonal to be good. Real giving considers both the receiver and the giver. The giver does not give to feel good but to help the person receiving the gift. What makes the gospel gift splendidly beautiful is that it is unknown and comes as close as it is possible to come to true, Christian radical altruism. Earth is not rich enough to reward such an act. The Father alone can and will give it a fitting reward: "Your Father who sees in secret will repay you."

Prayer will be judged in the same way. Christ insists on the Father's reward, personally given. Scripture says: "…pray to your Father in secret. And your Father who sees in secret will repay you." Matthew is far from saying that the Father is present only in the secret of one's room. God is everywhere.

This is the same Matthew who includes Christ's promise that "where two or three are gathered together in my name, there am I in the midst of them" (Matthew 18:20). Here, silence, solitude, and secrecy do not acquire value in themselves. They are prized because they reserve the act of prayer for God, who alone can reward such an act. Prayer is love in words and gives rise to love in action. Love and prayer go together like leaf and plant. One gives life to the other.

The English Romantic poet, Samuel Taylor Coleridge, wrote: "He prayeth best who loveth best / All things both great and small; / For the dear God who loveth us, / He made and loveth all." (*The Rime of the Ancient Mariner,* lines 610-617).

Fasting, likewise is valued not only for itself, but because it opens the spirit to the presence and action of God within the person. Fasting is a sign of one's desire to return to God. It is a sign of conversion, of a change of heart, therefore a sure sign that one is grasped by joy. A sad face, a droopy mien accompanying a fast is a contradiction. To seek out compassion and praise from people because of fasting is the ultimate nonsense. If the one who fasts thus is happy with the gazes and the pity of others, then the reward ends there. God alone repays the one who fasts, prays and gives alms. That is the joy of Lent and of life.

At La Salette, Mary chastises those who refuse to do penance: "*In Lent they go to the butcher shops like dogs.*" Penance and reconciliation go together like thirst and water: the need to show hunger for God, the urgency to express readiness to receive God erupts in the all-out generosity of fasting. Fasting is an extreme, a foolishness of the soul, an expression of longing for the loved one. Love is all of that too. That accounts for some of the Beautiful Lady's forthright words and the tears.

Reflection Questions:
• What habits of faith (almsgiving, prayer, fasting or other positive-action practices) have you performed in quiet during past Lenten seasons?

• Which habits of faith (daily or weekly Eucharist, the Sacrament of Reconciliation, Exposition of the Blessed Sacrament, or other practices) do you frequently perform "just for the love of God"?

Prayer:
Most Holy Mary, your reminder to us of some of the Lenten hab-

its of faith helps us reflect on how these practices that can strengthen our faith and deepen our devotion to your Son, who lived, suffered and died that we might have life to the full.

Through your intercession, may we remain faithful to daily prayer, the Eucharist, and other selfless Christian practices of love which can enrich our lives and keep our focus on Jesus, who died on the cross and rose to set us free. We ask this through your Son, who lives with the Father and the Holy Spirit, one God, for ever and ever. **Amen.**

Invocation:
Our Lady of La Salette, Reconciler of Sinners, pray without ceasing for us who have recourse to you.

Chapter Twelve:

"In Remembrance of Me"

Scripture: 1 Corinthians 11:23-26 (*The earliest account of the Institution of the Eucharist*)

> *I received from the Lord what I also handed on to you, that the Lord Jesus, on the night he was handed over, took bread, and, after he had given thanks, broke it and said, "This is my body that is for you. Do this in remembrance of me." In the same way also the cup, after supper, saying, "This cup is the new covenant in my blood. Do this, as often as you drink it, in remembrance of me." For as often as you eat this bread and drink the cup, you proclaim the death of the Lord until he comes.*

Reflection: This is a special moment in the ministry of Christ. St. Paul stresses the timing of the Lord's Supper: "…on the night he was handed over." He is about to leave them, or to be taken from them and this leave-taking meal assumes great importance and takes on a solemn mood. Many times while he was with his disciples, he told them how much he loved them. He expressed his affection for them in word and gesture. Now he thinks of leaving them a heartfelt departure gift: himself.

All the gospels, each one in its own fashion, stress the Lord's desire to be with his people. The supreme desire of the lover is to be with the beloved. One might say that in this case, Christ makes use of his power to bring about an expression of love never shown before in all of history. He has devised a way to be present to his friends throughout their lives on earth.

The manner of that presence is revealing. He will be with them as nourishment, a source of strength. It will be everlastingly renewable. The simplicity of the food – bread and wine – will make it available to everyone. This food is clearly not for physical growth. It is meant to nourish a special friendship, a relationship.

Christ is also clearly not foreseeing loneliness for his fledgling flock. This constant presence is meant to bring about a constant increase of love and intimacy. The Eucharist is a reminder to all the faithful that the Lord of the Living wants no part of long-distance protestations of affection. Not only does he want to be part of his disciples' lives; he wants to be their life.

He says, "This is my body that is for you." This simple sentence describes the whole idea of the Eucharist: it is for people. This is a gift completely and totally directed to another.

Surely, this marvelous act is not only meant to be received. The sheer generosity of it, the complete selflessness of it is meant to be emulated and imitated by those who receive it. As I receive this gift of a Person, so am I urged to give personally. As the gift is constantly available, so am I challenged to be constant gift. As the gift is complete, so am I called upon to give without conditions, clauses and fine print. As the gift is also a presence, so am I summoned to be an affirming, pleasant, discreet and compassionate presence to family and community. As the gift is given for the growth of friendship, so am I invited to remember those who love me, to be a faithful and understanding friend to those who are close to me.

To those who seek the secrets of love there is no greater legacy than this. You will never receive a more personal gift, nor a more "practical" one – Guaranteed for Life.

At La Salette, Mary is also concerned about the nourishment of "her children" – both their spiritual as well as physical nourishment. Her love and concern are all-embracing and touch every corner of their lives. First, she mentions the lack of potatoes and then speaks about the prospect of a great famine. The wheat will fail;

the walnut and grape crops, central to their local diet, are in danger.

Then she speaks about coming blessings *"if (her people) are converted..."* Her concern for the faith-life and physical health of her people is sincere and intense. Like her Son at the Last Supper, her people need to be fed spiritually as well as physically. Like her Son, she wants only good things for her people but first they must be reconciled with him. They must truly live their faith by taking advantage of those habits of faith which she lists: prayer, Eucharist, Lenten observances, and respect for the name and person of her Son.

Reflection Questions:
- Like Our Lord Jesus, how have you "fed the hungry", whether physically or spiritually?

- What have you done – whether physically or spiritually – in the recent past for those you love?

Prayer:
Mary, Concerned Mother of All Your People, we hear your message loud and clear. You are troubled about our physical and spiritual livelihood. We are not meant to be alone, lacking food or lacking the comfort of faith in your Son. You only want good things for your people.

Your Loving Son, in his marvelous gift of the Eucharist, was also concerned that his people be fed both physically as well as spiritually. And, like your Son, your love and concern at La Salette for your children were all-embracing and touched every corner of their lives. Through your intercession, guide us back to your Son, who lives with the Father and the Holy Spirit, one God, for ever and ever. **Amen.**

Invocation:
Our Lady of La Salette, Reconciler of Sinners, pray without ceasing for us who have recourse to you.

Chapter Thirteen:

Blood and Water

Scripture: John 19:25-37 (*The crucifixion of Jesus*)

...Standing by the cross of Jesus were his mother and his mother's sister, Mary the wife of Clopas, and Mary of Magdala. When Jesus saw his mother and the disciple there whom he loved, he said to his mother, "Woman, behold, your son." Then he said to the disciple, "Behold, your mother." And from that hour the disciple took her into his home.

After this, aware that everything was now finished, in order that the scripture might be fulfilled, Jesus said, "I thirst."

The Deposition by Caravaggio (1571 - 1610)

There was a vessel filled with common wine. So they put a sponge soaked in wine on a sprig of hyssop and put it up to his mouth. When Jesus had taken the wine, he said, "It is finished." And bowing his head, he handed over the spirit.

Now since it was preparation day, in order that the bodies might not remain on the cross on the sabbath, for the sabbath day of that week was a solemn one, the Jews asked Pilate that their legs be broken and they be taken down. So the soldiers came and broke the legs of the first and then of the other one who was crucified with Jesus. But when they came to Jesus and saw that he was already dead, they did not break his legs, but one soldier thrust his lance into his side, and immediately blood and water flowed out.

An eyewitness has testified, and his testimony is true; he knows that he is speaking the truth, so that you also may [come to] believe. For this happened so that the scripture passage might be fulfilled: "Not a bone of it will be broken." And again another passage says: "They will look upon him whom they have pierced."

Reflection: The Passion of Christ as it is found in our four gospels is not only a recital of events in the final moments of the life of Christ on earth. It is also an instruction, a preaching, a living example given to the world of the total gift of himself that Christ gave to the world.

For anyone even somewhat gifted with words, it is possible, on a given Good Friday, to elicit tears by recalling the sound of flailing whips drawing bloody stripes on the back of Christ, the spray of spittle assaulting his face, the brutish swat of hands slapping his head. Pity, heart-felt pity surfaces in the soul of any sensitive listener. Indeed, this scenario would draw compassion from any sensitive person no matter who the victim might be.

But the gospel proclaimed on Good Friday reminds us that this is God being spat upon, whipped, slapped. This is the blood of God reddening the back of God. This is God dying, the Master of the life in the universe, dying out of love for all that is human. St. John tells us, as God hung on the cross, what was happening at Christ's feet.

Someone was readying an inscription to be nailed over the head of the victim: "Jesus the Nazarean, the King of the Jews" (John:19:21), it said. It was written in Latin, Hebrew and Greek, the three languages spoken in the world of that time. St. John looks at these words as a statement of fact more than an accusation. Jesus was, indeed, the King of the Jews and of the whole world.

The soldiers stripped Christ of his clothes and they cast lots to see who would get his tunic. If the death had been glorious, if he had died as a hero for a national cause, his dignity might have been salvaged. But Christ lost his life and also his "face" in ridicule and with the jeering laughter of the soldiers still echoing in his ears. They had placed the mocking purple mantle on him in derision, and now in mockery they stripped him.

Meanwhile, his mother and the disciple whom Jesus loved stood at the foot of the cross. Thinking of his mother in this awful hour, he gave her to the beloved disciple as a mother to care for and he gave the disciple to her as a son.

The gospel of John never calls Mary by her name. He always gives her the title of mother, as if to stress the power and dignity of that title. The Church has from the beginning interpreted this scene as Christ's gift of Mary to his people as their mother.

In John, chapter 13, we read: "He loved his own in the world and he loved them to the end." (John 13:1). This "end" can mean the end of Christ's life; and it can also signify the limit, the furthest reaches of his heart and strength. John seems to have left the meaning purposely undetermined.

Now, after drinking the sour wine from the hyssop that had been raised to his lips, he said, "It is finished." This is the "end" that the gospel writer alluded to earlier. We, who have been graced by this life and this death can claim – as someone said – that we have never been Christ's *hobby*, but rather his *lifelong passion*.

The soldiers who had crucified Jesus were satisfied that he was dead but they still gave him one last injury. "…one soldier thrust his lance into his side, and immediately blood and water flowed out." In death there was life. In John's "sign language", water stands for the Spirit and blood for life.

As a result of the death of the Lord, his people receive his Spirit and this Spirit is the giver of life, the very life of Christ. Indeed, the Lord had given all of himself – his heart and his soul. He had given up the earthly success of his mission as well as his good name. In the end, there remained only blood and water, and they were enough.

The crucifix on the Lady's breast at La Salette is more than a symbol. He is the "Son" she mentions three times in her discourse. He is the center of her life; he is her life. She had given him his body, his humanity. She had given him the blood he had shed on Calvary. The Lady who had stood on Calvary now stands at La Salette. She was called "mother" on Calvary and this was to prove more than a mere title. On the other mountain at La Salette, she weeps still, up to this very day, for all her people – for each and every one of them.

Reflection Questions:
- When have you "comforted the sorrowing"?
- When have you help others to bear their cross?

Prayer:
Mary, Mother of the Savior, your tears of grief at the death of your Son on the cross are a testament to your love for your only Son. Your tears at La Salette are also an evidence of your concern for all your people.

Through your ceaseless prayers for us, assist on our own journey of faith back to the Father. Guide us by your words and example at La Salette to be true disciples of your Son, who lives with the Father and the Holy Spirit, one God, for ever and ever. **Amen.**

Invocation:
Our Lady of La Salette, Reconciler of Sinners, pray without ceasing for us who have recourse to you.

Chapter Fourteen:

The Joy of the Bridegroom

Scripture: Matthew 9:14-15 (*The question about fasting*)

When Jesus had crossed in the territory of the Gerasenes, the disciples of John approached him and said, "Why do we and the Pharisees fast [much], but your disciples do not fast?" Jesus answered them, "Can the wedding guests mourn as long as the bridegroom is with them? The days will come when the bridegroom is taken away from them, and then they will fast."

Reflection: The gospel brings a great truth to the fore: we make use of human faculties to express the depth of our faith. The disciples of John were surprised that those of Christ did not fast as much they did. John's disciples were meticulous observers of an exhausting fast. (They discreetly abstained from bringing Jesus into the picture; they only mentioned his disciples.)

Jesus mentioned nothing about the practice of fasting. He goes beyond it. For Jews and John's disciples, fasting and gloom were related. Christ refers to a time of joy and this time is the present. He associates his presence with his disciples as a time of elation and delight. The disciples of John as well as the Pharisees associated fasting with sadness and mourning. Christ sees himself as bringing happiness to his own.

This passage harmonizes well with Matthew's general argument that Christ is ever-present to his people. We remember his choice of the Immanuel prophecy as a central issue in the life of Christ.

We remember his promise, "For where two or three are gathered together in my name, there I am in the midst of them" (Matthew 18:20).

In the parable of the last judgment, Christ not only associates himself with the hungry and the thirsty and the naked but identifies with them, "for one of these least... of mine, you did for me" (Matthew 25:40b). His presence makes a saving, joyful difference in a person's life.

In this reading Christ states outright: "Can the wedding guests mourn as long as the bridegroom is with them?" (Matthew 9:15). That "cannot" is a brawny ban on gloom. To be sad in the presence of Christ the bridegroom makes as much sense as a wedding dirge. This is not an opinion voiced by some disciples. It is Christ who says this.

The fast of our yearly season is not a melancholy exercise in self-immolation. It is a statement by the followers of Christ that they want to follow him more closely, enter his life more completely. Fasting is as joyful as the bridegroom's eagerness to please his bride.

Sad faces, sad gaits, ashen miens do not merge well with what the church calls the "joyful season of Lent." In this reading Christ proclaims that discipleship is not grim, that religion (being "linked" to him, which is what true religion is) should not be bleak and black.

Indeed, one concludes that an habitually morose and gloomy mien indicates a misunderstanding of religion. Why indeed would Christ choose a wedding situation to express this idea?

The tearful Lady of La Salette may have been forthright about people going to the butcher shops *"like dogs"*, but for those who *"are converted, rocks and stones will turn into heaps of wheat, and potatoes will be self-sown in the fields."* These generous Messianic promises all refer to food.

The Lady agrees with her Son: religion caters to the whole person, both spirit and body. There is no Christ and no discipleship without human joy.

Reflection Questions:
- What person do you know who needs God's help to come to an active faith?

- Whom do you admire as a truly joyful person?

Prayer:
Mary, Joyful Queen of Heaven, your tears belie the joy you find in visiting your people and reminding them of their call to make your message known. Your prophetic words can distract us from your underlying motivation to save your needy people and bring them back to the ways and message of your Son.

As you stood with a tearful countenance, your words nevertheless were filled with the hope and concern of a mother calling her children back to new life. Through your intercession, may your most generous invitation be welcomed by more of your people. And may they find true and lasting happiness in making your message known to all your people. We ask this through your loving Son, who lives with the Father and the Holy Spirit, one God, for ever and ever. **Amen.**

Invocation:
Our Lady of La Salette, Reconciler of Sinners, pray without ceasing for us who have recourse to you.

Part Four:
God's Compassion, Mercy, and Healing

Chapter Fifteen:

The Lord of Life and Burdens Light

Scripture: Matthew 11:28-30 (*The gentle mastery of Christ*)

> *Jesus said to the crowds: "Come to me, all you who labor and are burdened, and I will give you rest. Take my yoke upon you and learn from me, for I am meek and humble of heart; and you will find rest for yourselves. For my yoke is easy, and my burden light."*

Reflection: In this apparently sermon-like brief passage, Jesus boldly reveals who he really is. If there was ever a doubt before these words were uttered, there had to be no doubt afterward.

It was common currency for the scribes and the Pharisees to recommend Wisdom and for the Rabbis to refer their own to the splendors of the Law for the proper pursuit of their lives.

Christ made more than a symbolic statement that day. He gave forth a way of life, an attitude, a philosophy and a sure way to genuine personal peace. When he declared, "Come to me," he canceled out every other manner of living, every other avenue to comfort and strength.

He seemed to be speaking to a specific category of people on that occasion: "all you who labor and are burdened", but I would dare say that every one of us qualifies as weary and burdened in some way, even if some are more so than others. Very likely, and more specifically, the burdens alluded to here are the weighty demands of the Law, the many precepts and demands of a legalism that had crept into every area of life.

Perhaps the Lord's boldest statement is, "and I will give you rest." He did not say I will give you the means, the strategies of peace and contentment, but that he, Jesus, would give them rest. We recall his declaration in the gospel of John, "I am the way and the truth and the life" (John 14:6). Christ comes to earth and becomes the good news, the joy of salvation that has to be a counterweight to the tough demands of the Law.

No one was doing away with moral law and the demands of living together in harmony, but Christ was bringing hope and a vision of the future where he himself would be the long-awaited bliss.

The common expectation of the Messiah at the time of Jesus was of an all-conquering hero who would free Israel from its captivity. Gentleness and meekness were not as prized as the vision of a macho Messiah. Still, the prophets did not forget his humility: "Exult greatly, O daughter Zion! Shout for joy, O daughter Jerusalem! Behold: your king is coming to you, a just savior is he, Humble, and riding on a donkey, on a colt, the foal of a donkey" (Zechariah 9:9). There are many ways of being strong and the Son of God chooses to be perceived as gentle and meek.

Christ says that "my yoke is easy, and my burden light" (Matthew 11:30). The burdens and the yokes of each follower is measured according to the capacity of the bearer. In the days of Christ, yokes were fitted to the neck and contours of each individual animal. Thus the yoke was made easy, appropriate, and adapted to each one. These are words worth remembering, especially in times of turmoil and sadness, when the heart is flooded with pain and no human hand can relieve the weight of anguish. This reading proclaims the Christ-centered life.

At La Salette, the Weeping Mother appeared and spoke especially of her Son. She pronounces the word "Son" five times. On her breast, the crucified Christ is in bright and shimmering evidence.

This is a suffering Christ, who in some way, still bears the burden of the cross. The mother herself says clearly, *"How long have I suffered for you!"*

The mother and the Son, though in heaven, are still, in some mysterious but real way, burdened with suffering. Yet, the reason for her visit at La Salette is peace. If there is reconciliation, this same Son will bring with his own presence in the world, a Messianic abundance: *"rocks and stones will turn into heaps of wheat, and potatoes will be self-sown in the fields."*

La Salette is filled with the gospel invitation: "Come to me, all you who labor and are burdened."

Reflection Questions:
- When has Jesus (or another person) "made our burdens light"?
- When has someone asked you to help they by lifting their burdens?

Prayer:
Mary, Mother of Comfort, you know well that your children often are called to bear the extra burdens of life amid the normal responsibilities of daily living. In order to cope with all these needs, we must have your Son as the center of our life. He is the Prince of Peace and can assist us in ways only available through his grace.

As the center of your life, you depend on him for the ability to be patient with and pray constantly for his people – your people. Through your intercession, assist us in allowing ourselves to rest in the loving arms of your Son. We ask this through the same Jesus, who lives with the Father and the Holy Spirit, one God, for ever and ever. **Amen**.

Invocation:
Our Lady of La Salette, Reconciler of Sinners, pray without ceasing for us who have recourse to you.

Chapter Sixteen:

Believing Because He Saw

Scripture: John 4:43-54 (*The second sign at Cana*)

Jesus left (Samaria) for Galilee. For Jesus himself testified that a prophet has no honor in his native place. When he came into Galilee, the Galileans welcomed him, since they had seen all he had done in Jerusalem at the feast; for they themselves had gone to the feast.

Then he returned to Cana in Galilee, where he had made the water wine. Now there was a royal official whose son was ill in Capernaum. When he heard that Jesus had arrived in Galilee from Judea, he went to him and asked him to come down and heal his son, who was near death. Jesus said to him, "Unless you people see signs and wonders, you will not believe." The royal official said to him, "Sir, come down before my child dies." Jesus said to him, "You may go; your son will live." The man believed what Jesus said to him and left.

While he was on his way back, his slaves met him and told him that his boy would live. He asked them when he began to recover. They told him, "The fever left him yesterday, about one in the afternoon." The father realized that just at that time Jesus had said to him, "Your son will live," and he and his whole household came to believe. [Now] this was the second sign Jesus did when he came to Galilee from Judea.

Reflection: John's gospel is a hymn to faith. The vocabulary of faith, trust, and belief is more common in this gospel than that of love. The miracle we witness in this passage is the "second sign Jesus did." All the signs written about in this gospel concern faith. At the close of his work, John writes that all of these signs "are written so that you may come to believe that Jesus is the Messiah, the Son of God, and that through this belief you may have life in his name" (John 20:31). The miracle of the royal official's son is all about faith and all about life.

In previous encounters with seekers of faith, Christ had spoken to Nicodemus, "who had come to Jesus at night" (John 3:2) and had come to faith with doubt and hesitation. Nicodemus was the typical Jew but the Samaritan woman whom Jesus met at the well was neither Jew nor pagan. She came to faith a little more quickly and perhaps more enthusiastically than Nicodemus after Jesus had revealed to her that she had had five husbands. She believed and she brought all her village with her to the faith.

The royal official was neither Jew nor Samaritan. He was the typical pagan and he came to faith quickly and we might initially suspect that his word of faith was self-serving. Was it the 'smart' or clever thing to do? After all he was in urgent personal need. His son was deathly sick and this was no time for discussion.

But John leads us to think that indeed there was too much at stake to simulate trust. This man ranked high in more than political power. He appears to be of noble heart. His faith in Jesus is immediate and implicit. John has a singular and simple way of describing the official's faith. The official believed so completely that he simply started on his way home. The cure was as good as accomplished. He was intelligent enough to realize that anyone who could cure his little son could do so without being present.

What is special about this cure is that there is life involved. Human life restored becomes a symbol of everlasting life given through faith. Life was restored through the faith of the father.

In the Nicodemus story there was the life of the spirit and renewal through water and the Spirit. At Cana, water had been changed into wine. But, at the well, the Samaritan woman saw water become a symbol of life. Christ himself came into another person's life as gift.

But in the three cases of Nicodemus, of the woman at the well, of the cure of the royal official's son, all came to faith and to life because they had met Jesus. They had become witnesses to faith and life because they had come to know him. Clearly then, the source of faith is the Lord himself. He creates the gift and grants it to individuals.

It is a dream of a gift because it brings people into the very life of God. It is a dream of earthly life also because it changes human life and leads it, in a quantum bound, into another sphere which enriches the life each one lives on earth.

Faith is a gift for all people. In these three episodes, there is the upper-class Jew, a member of a powerful institution, the Sanhedrin. There is a woman who had had many husbands and whose life was a shambles. She could have expected to meet Jesus that day as much as one could expect to see God at a well. Then there was the pagan, an outsider with a sick child, and his entire household. Grace is ecumenical, and universal. It seeks both genders and all ages, all states of life and power and wealth. The gift of faith brings the gift of the hospitable heart.

At La Salette, Mary said, "*Well, my children, you will make it known to all my people.*" By the ministry of Maximin and Melanie, her words would stir the Church but go beyond it to the whole world. The entire world is thus called to faith and life. The gospel of John is predicated on faith, on the belief that the love of God for all people is not something one can understand. Only faith can grasp it. The Lady weeps at La Salette for all the people who do not know the beauty of faith which is an aspect of God's love for people.

Reflection Questions:
- Whom do you know who has "a noble heart", and a solid life of faith?

- When has your faith in God carried you through some difficulties?

Prayer:
Mary, Trusting Mother of the Savior, your choice of Maximin and Melanie was as surprising as it was wise beyond imagining. It was a tremendously trusting invitation to two ordinary and unsuspecting children to spread your message of faith and reconciliation to all your people. Your Son also chose his disciples, and he now calls us, his needy people, to do the same.

May your Son increase our faith and direct our lives that we may be faithful to your call to make your message known. We ask this through your loving Son, who lives with the Father and the Holy Spirit, one God, for ever and ever. **Amen.**

Invocation:
Our Lady of La Salette, Reconciler of Sinners, pray without ceasing for us who have recourse to you.

Chapter Seventeen:

The Blind Men Who Caught Up to Christ

Scripture: Matthew 9:27-31 (*The healing of two blind men*)

As Jesus passed by, two blind men followed him, crying out, "Son of David, have pity on us!" When he entered the house, the blind men approached him and Jesus said to them, "Do you believe that I can do this?" "Yes, Lord," they said to him. Then he touched their eyes and said, "Let it be done for you according to your faith." And their eyes were opened. Jesus warned them sternly, "See that no one knows about this." But they went out and spread word of him through all that land.

Reflection: Reading the gospels for any length of time in one sitting, one is struck with the image of Christ as a pursued man. Sought out is not the word. Stalked, tracked and trailed would be more appropriate. This rabbi could really heal and cure. People who couldn't walk began jumping up and down; people who couldn't talk began speaking; people, whose blood gushed out in streams, stopped bleeding.

Bartimaeus had to scream after Christ and the two blind men in our reading "followed him crying out, 'Son of David, have pity on us!'" Apparently the Lord did not hear them for a while. "When he entered the house, the blind men approached him." Here was someone who could restore sight and he was passing through the area and they were determined not to miss him.

Upon hearing the gospel, one is also left with the impression that all those who asked to be healed got better. Whenever Christ was stricken with pity, he responded to that call to pity. He passed through one village after another and people expected him, waited for him, and did not want to miss him.

They were not only impressed with his power over illness but also with what he had to tell them as well as by his manner of speaking. If they were hale of mind and body, they received something for the spirit. They heard truth when he spoke of God the Father, of God's kindness, and endless forgiveness.

In all he said and did, Christ had one purpose in mind, one single overriding goal: to reveal the Father. He was the revelation of the Father. And this Father was one who had the heart to heal and cure and speak marvelous words of comfort and truth. Christ revealed a God who wanted – very much wanted – to be present to people, both in the individuality of their suffering and in their sharing in a community.

Healing, speaking with people and to them, eating and feasting with them, rejoicing and suffering with them, Christ was telling individuals and crowds that this was the type of God that had made them and whom they were now serving. No wonder they ran after Christ, after healing, faith, mercy and forgiveness. They were running after God.

Mary at La Salette came to imitate her Son in what he had done and to share his mission. She showed the world the suffering of an abandoned Lord. She revealed, if it had to be revealed, that in some mysterious way, God grieves and weeps for people. It is nothing less than stirring to see that at La Salette, the Lord wanted to let us know that God is indeed caring for his people to the point of tears.

The children, Maximin and Melanie, whose acquaintance with God was a nodding one at best, knew all this instinctively. The two blind men pursued Christ, and at La Salette the children ran up the hillock after the Lady as she was about to disappear. They did not want her to leave. In a single half-hour, they had learned to love her. And thus it is with all who run after him with open hearts. They run after God until God captures them.

Reflection Questions:
- What words, actions or attitudes during Mary's visit at La Salette recall some qualities shown in the life of her Son?

- Do you know anyone whose life was profoundly changed when they began to believe in God?

Prayer:
Mary, Mother of Christ, your compassionate visit with the two children of La Salette shows not only your own heart but also that of your Son. In supporting your visit on that Holy Mountain, your Son wanted us to know that God is indeed caring for his people to the point of tears.

Your words and actions are a clear reminder that Jesus wishes to heal our wounds, forgive our sins, and give us life in his name. Through your intercession, hear our prayer that we may continue to be open to his grace of reconciliation and share it readily with others. We ask this through your loving Son, who lives with the Father and the Holy Spirit, one God, for ever and ever. **Amen**.

Invocation:
Our Lady of La Salette, Reconciler of Sinners, pray without ceasing for us who have recourse to you.

Chapter Eighteen:

The Reign of God is Here

Scripture: Matthew 9:35 to 10:1,6-8 (*The compassion of Jesus and the commissioning of the Twelve*)

Jesus went around to all the towns and villages, teaching in their synagogues, proclaiming the Gospel of the Kingdom, and curing every disease and illness. At the sight of the crowds, his heart was moved with pity for them because they were troubled and abandoned, like sheep without a shepherd. Then he said to his disciples, "The harvest is abundant but the laborers are few; so ask the master of the harvest to send out laborers for his harvest." Then he summoned his Twelve disciples and gave them authority over unclean spirits to drive them out and to cure every disease and every illness.

Jesus sent out these Twelve after instructing them thus, "Go to the lost sheep of the house of Israel. As you go, make this proclamation: 'The Kingdom of heaven is at hand.' Cure the sick, raise the dead, cleanse lepers, drive out demons. Without cost you have received; without cost you are to give."

Reflection: Reading the gospels, one sometimes gets the feeling that the Lord is in a hurry. He appears to have drawn up a plan of action, an agenda, and he is racing against time to fulfill it. Apparently he is reaching out to as many people as possible. Jesus was eager to tell people about the Father but it was not to be mere advertising. All of these meetings with people would be quality, face-to-face encounters. "Jesus went around to all the towns and villages, teaching in their synagogues, proclaiming the Gospel of the Kingdom."

He would send disciples but he insisted on seeing as many people as possible. When Jesus could, he saw them where they lived. He would talk to them, heal them, eat with them, and "At the sight of the crowds, his heart was moved with pity for them because they were troubled and abandoned." At times, he saw all the work he had to do, he witnessed all the good will he had to harness and we detect a tone of impatience with the task, "The harvest is abundant but the laborers are few."

Upon reflection, we stand surprised to learn how intensely and deeply God wants people to know about him. At the end of this gospel of Matthew, Jesus gave one last command to the disciples gathered around him, "Go, therefore, and make disciples of all nations" (Matthew 28:19). Once again, we stand before a mystery that can only be the mystery of God's affection for people. Why make himself known to us? Why insist that we love him? Why all those divine declarations of fidelity and affection?

And the mystery deepens. God doesn't want a mere passing acquaintance with people. He doesn't want a casual relationship. The purpose is not to increase the number of individuals or nations who know God so that he can rack up numbers and percentages. God's reason for preaching God is that he wants a relationship to be born and to thrive between himself and individuals. He wants to be part of the lives of individuals, part of their joys and pain, part of their entire human experience.

The Word became flesh not as an achievement to be recorded by the Godhead, but as desire to become one with other humans, to know what it means to have blood coursing in the veins of God and to have people see what God looks like when he smiles as well as when he weeps.

When he left the human world, he arranged to have others make him known. "Then he summoned his Twelve disciples and gave them authority over unclean spirits to drive them out and to cure every disease and every illness." Henceforth, people who knew about God would know that God heals, liberates, forgives, abides, is loyal, loves. The people who would make him known best would be the people who loved him most.

At La Salette, Mary chose a tiny, remote village high up in the Alps in which to appear. She probably meant to convey the notion that small villages and little people also dwell in the heart of God. In human assessment, very few villages were smaller than the village of La Salette and few people were smaller than Maximin and Melanie.

And we know how she won their hearts and their lifelong loyalty. We know how everything else they saw and heard in life was compared to that Saturday afternoon on the mountain and everything and everyone fell short. At the end of her apparition she said, "*Well, my children, you will make it known to all my people*". And she stressed and insisted on that, "*Well my children,*" she said a second time, "*you will make it known to all my people.*"

Once again God wanted us all to know and to realize that God was still present among people. That these people were "God's people". He sent two children as messengers, a humanly absurd idea and a more ludicrous choice of witnesses. Now the world knows how well they fulfilled their mission. La Salette is an act of love, and act of presence to humankind. Through La Salette, God says to all of us, "I am still here and I care as much as ever about you." After many centuries, Christ is still in a hurry.

Reflection Questions:
- When have you reached out in compassion to the needs of another?

- In being confronted with the deep needs of another person, when have you hesitated or even decided not to help them – even for some good reason?

Prayer:
Mary, Mother of Compassion, your Son's example of pity for his troubled people is mirrored in your words and actions at La Salette. Your thoughtful mention of the Maximin's father's fear of not being able to provide food for his family touched your heart and urged you to remind Maximin of that sad event in the field of Coin.

Through your intercession, may your Son continue to touch and change our hearts. May we, in turn, reach out in compassion to those who need to feel the concern your Son has for them and their loved ones. We ask this through your Son, who lives with the Father and the Holy Spirit, one God, for ever and ever. **Amen.**

Invocation:
Our Lady of La Salette, Reconciler of Sinners, pray without ceasing for us who have recourse to you.

Part Five: Love and Service

Chapter Nineteen:

Portrait of the Neighbor

Scripture: Matthew 5:20-26 (*Teaching about anger*)

Jesus said to his disciples: I tell you, unless your righteousness surpasses that of the scribes and Pharisees, you will not enter into the kingdom of heaven. "You have heard that it was said to your ancestors, 'You shall not kill; and whoever kills will be liable to judgment.' But I say to you, whoever is angry with his brother will be liable to judgment, and whoever says to his brother, 'Raqa,' will be answerable to the Sanhedrin, and whoever says, 'You fool,' will be liable to fiery Gehenna.

Therefore, if you bring your gift to the altar, and there recall that your brother has anything against you, leave your gift there at the altar, go first and be reconciled with your brother, and then come and offer your gift.

Settle with your opponent quickly while on the way to court with him. Otherwise your opponent will hand you over to the judge, and the judge will hand you over to the guard, and you will be thrown into prison. Amen, I say to you, you will not be released until you have paid the last penny.

Reflection: We have no portrait of Christ, no likeness to reveal his physical characteristics. What we have is the portrait of his mind, his thinking. This is of paramount importance since it is so intimately related to the teaching of the New Testament and, for the Christian, to personal justice and salvation. People have often asked Christ what is the most important feature of his teaching.

In every instance it is discipleship of Christ through love of neighbor. Christ insists everywhere that the Christian spirit exists only in this anchor and linchpin of his teaching. If Christ can be said to have an obsession, a favored and ever-recurring one in his preaching, this is it (Mt 19:16; Mk 10:17; Lk 10:25; 18,18; 1 Jn 4:7-12). The New Testament landscape is covered with these signposts of justice and salvation. Overt or implied, this is a leitmotif, a ubiquitous and pervasive proviso.

Our passage illustrates this very well. It also gives a few lessons on how to go about doing it, which is a different matter altogether.

This teaching is lofty stuff but Christ's words are at ground level. "You have heard that it was said to your ancestors, 'You shall not kill... But I say to you, whoever is angry with his brother will be liable to judgment." Love and affection surface in behavior. It is not enough to respect the neighbor's legal rights. Christ reaches into the heart, the place of anger and of love.

This is where the love of neighbor is first violated. Trying to live out one's religion without kindness and respect for the neighbor is like wanting to breathe without air. Worship is skewed not only when we come to the altar harboring resentment against the neighbor but also when the neighbor has something against us.

We learn that reconciliation with a brother or sister has two features: first, it does not matter who is to blame for the initial misunderstanding or discord; whoever wishes to approach the altar must first attempt to reestablish peace and concord. Secondly, this attempt must be quick and real: "Settle with your opponent quickly while on the way to court with him."

This is what happened at La Salette. The injured party took the initiative of reconciliation. Christ sent his Mother to earth with conciliatory advances. The message was pointed, realistic with words as clear as mountain water. The Lady clearly brought out discordant issues and provided the terms for a prompt reconciliation. But, realistic as it was, it was spoken to the accompaniment of tears.

For reasons that escape us, God "missed" our closeness; God wanted a renewed friendship and a deepened intimacy. The motive should not really escape us, though. This reconciliation means much to both Mother and Son. To discover how much this means to them, we need but to think that the Son has shed all of his blood while his Mother continues to shed her tears.

Reflection Questions:
- When have you been called to ask forgiveness of your neighbor?
- When have you been called to forgive your neighbor?

Prayer:
Mary, Mother Most Merciful, you were sent by your Son to La Salette to reconcile us to ourselves, to our neighbor and to God. And your words were accompanied by the language of your tears, poignantly reflecting the sorrow of your Son for his people. Your Son's emphasis on the absolute necessity of his followers to commit to love of God, neighbor, and self was the hallmark of his ministry.

Through your intercession, keep before our minds and hearts this loving mandate of sharing your message of reconciliation with everyone we meet. We ask this through the grace of your loving Son, who lives with the Father and the Holy Spirit, one God, for ever and ever. **Amen.**

Invocation:
Our Lady of La Salette, Reconciler of Sinners, pray without ceasing for us who have recourse to you.

Chapter Twenty:

I Do Not Wish to Send Them Away Hungry

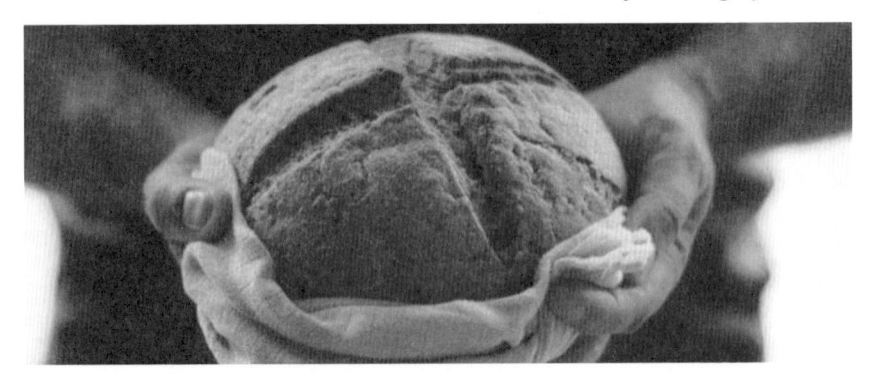

Scripture: Matthew 15:29-37 (*The healing of many people and the feeding of the four thousand*)

Moving on from there Jesus walked by the Sea of Galilee, went up on the mountain, and sat down there. Great crowds came to him, having with them the lame, the blind, the deformed, the mute, and many others. They placed them at his feet, and he cured them. The crowds were amazed when they saw the mute speaking, the deformed made whole, the lame walking, and the blind able to see, and they glorified the God of Israel.

Jesus summoned his disciples and said, "My heart is moved with pity for the crowd, for they have been with me now for three days and have nothing to eat. I do not want to send them away hungry, for fear they may collapse on the way." The disciples said to him, "Where could we ever get enough bread in this deserted place to satisfy such a crowd?"

Jesus said to them, "How many loaves do you have?" "Seven," they replied, "and a few fish." He ordered the crowd to sit down on the ground. Then he took the seven loaves and the fish, gave thanks, broke the loaves, and gave them to the disciples, who in turn gave them to the crowds. They all ate and were satisfied. They picked up the fragments left over – seven baskets full.

Reflection: The gospels tell their story with more than one purpose in mind. They tell of the ministry of Jesus to the people of his time and these stories become more than stories but calls to the people of all time to learn what kind of Person this Christ is.

Matthew multiplies the types of illnesses that Christ dealt with and this leads us to imagine that there were many more than he names here. These cures are visibly physical and they hint at the message that Christ also came to save people from diseases of the spirit and of the soul. Christ loved people and used his power to alleviate suffering, and this is called belaboring the obvious. The clear message is that God simply does not like to see people suffer.

The gospel shows us something unique about the heart of Christ. Whenever he is "moved with pity" in the presence of suffering, he acts on this pity. This is not easy-chair love and theoretical concern. It was not to prove his power that he produced food out of nowhere, but because "they have been with me three days, and have nothing to eat. I do not want to send them away hungry, for fear they may collapse on the way."

There is strong, implied praise of Christ here. The disciples make a point of saying that this is a huge crowd and there is precious little food at hand. When Jesus inquires, the disciples tell him that all they have is seven loaves of bread and a few small fish.

Christ takes the initiative. Christ is aware. The gospel shows us a Christ who is alert to conditions and situations, to people around him. He may be prayerful and contemplative, but he is not asleep.

This miracle underlines Christ's generosity. It is characteristic of God that he never gives just enough, except perhaps to prove a point. He deals in abundant and overwhelming gifts. Matthew makes sure we know that: "They all ate and were satisfied."

One is left with the impression that possessive skimping is abhorrent to him. He deals in open-handed magnanimity and gives new meaning to "largesse". "They picked up the fragments left over – seven baskets full." This crowd was not to go home hungry.

At La Salette Mary reminded the world that Christ has not fallen asleep. The poverty of the village of La Salette in 1846 gave misery a bad name. People were utterly poor: poor in morale, in piety, in food and in money. The Lady shed tears and revealed that nineteen centuries after the resurrection, God was still "moved with pity." He was awake and caring enough to send his mother to the people of the world.

The message of La Salette points out ills and threatens in order to heal. But time has not changed the heart of a generous Lord. *"If they are converted, rocks and stones will turn into heaps of wheat, and potatoes will be self-sown in the fields."*

Seven hampers of left-over food in the Lord's miracle, people healed of all manner of illnesses and diseases, stones turned into heaps of wheat and self-sown potatoes: we are dealing here with Someone who wants to protect His reputation for munificence. Promises, threats, healings, cures, abounding food, tears – a lot happens before the *"arm of my Son"* comes down.

But that also is done out of love.

Reflection Questions:
- When have you been touched to the heart and drawn to act at the need of another?

- When have you seen another respond to someone's desperate situation?

Prayer:
Mary, Mother of Mercy, your heart went out to these two poor children on that Holy Mountain. They were frail, surprised children who noticed your profound sadness and were drawn to you by your loving invitation to come near.

Draw us closer, Mary, to your loving Son. May we be inspired to feed others by our words and actions, our generosity and compassion, as you fed your two witnesses and us during your merciful visit at La Salette. We ask this through your intercession and through the grace of your loving Son, who lives with the Father and the Holy Spirit, one God, for ever and ever. **Amen**.

Invocation:
Our Lady of La Salette, Reconciler of Sinners, pray without ceasing for us who have recourse to you.

Chapter Twenty-One:

The Waters of Life

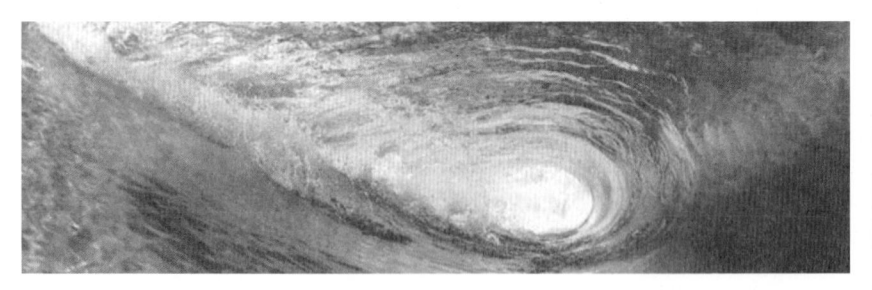

Scripture: John 7:40-52 (*Discussion about the origins of the Messiah*)

Some in the crowd who heard these words of Jesus said, "This is truly the Prophet." Others said, "This is the Messiah." But others said, "The Messiah will not come from Galilee, will he? Does not scripture say that the Messiah will be of David's family and come from Bethlehem, the village where David lived?" So a division occurred in the crowd because of him.

Some of them even wanted to arrest him, but no one laid hands on him. So the guards went to the chief priests and Pharisees, who asked them, "Why did you not bring him?" The guards answered, "Never before has anyone spoken like this one." So the Pharisees answered them, "Have you also been deceived? Have any of the authorities or the Pharisees believed in him? But this crowd, which does not know the law, is accursed."

Nicodemus, one of their members who had come to him earlier, said to them, "Does our law condemn a person before it first hears him and finds out what he is doing?" They answered and said to him, "You are not from Galilee also, are you? Look and see that no prophet arises from Galilee."

Reflection: Water flows abundantly in the life and ministry of

Christ. He changed water into wine as his first miracle and the first sign of his mission. He spoke to Nicodemus on that famous evening and told him of "being born of water and Spirit." He met the woman at the well in Samaria and asked her for a drink of water. He told her that if she had asked him, "he would have given you living water."

We now meet Christ at one of the great Jewish feasts. There were three great celebrations: the Feast of Tabernacles, or Booths; the Feast of Weeks and the Feast of Unleavened Bread. The Feast of Booths was the most important. It recalled the former days of harvest time in the fields when farmers would pitch tents of branches near the fields and live in them.

This Feast of Booths – or Tents, or Tabernacles – recalled these former times as an era of faith and fidelity to a provident God. How appropriate it was on this greatest feast to pray for rain and an abundant harvest for the coming year. We have to understand the crucial role of water in the mind of Christ's contemporaries to grasp the events described in this gospel.

A few verses before, John states that: "Jesus stood up and exclaimed, 'Let anyone who thirsts come to me and drink'" (John 7:37b). John adds that Jesus "said this in reference to the Spirit that those who came to believe in him were to receive" (John 7:39). This kind of talk had to make an impression on people who looked upon water as white gold and the stuff of life itself. They said, "Never before has anyone spoken like this one" (John 7:46).

The spirit of God was associated with water in the Hebrew bible. At the creation, a mighty wind or spirit, was: "sweeping over the waters" (Genesis 1:2).

Water was life. Christ was revealing himself as one who brought the Spirit of God, the Spirit of life to the world. No wonder they thought that no one had ever spoken like this. No one had spoken like this because no one could do what this man could do, nor give what he could give.

It is indeed quite amazing when someone can give a gift so astonishing that no one believes he can give it or that he does not have it to give. That gift is of such proportions that anyone saying he has it to give makes himself equal to God. People did not know what to make of him. Some thought he was a prophet. The police would not lay a finger on him.

The gospel reminds its readers that this is the man who matters most in their lives because he does not only give life, he is life. It tells them that this Christ is not only a great factor in their lives; he is the *only one*. The people in the gospel are confused because they don't know what to make of him.

Those who come to believe and trust have started on the path to peace. They begin to "get it all together" in their souls and in their lives when they meet with him and discover that he is their friend. The gift he can give them is *life*. What could be more important? That life is perceived in the gospel as water and Christ gives that gift to all.

At La Salette, the Lady appeared near a fountain that flowed intermittently. Prior to the apparition, it depended on the rains and the melting of snows. Since the apparition in 1846, this little brook has never stopped flowing. The Lady has adopted the humble symbol of water as a source of life, as her Son had done.

The Lady has long ago disappeared and the children of La Salette have gone, too, but the water flows on, a reminder that she spoke in the name of life. That water is a gift given at God's own initiative, abundantly, and its flow still has not ended. We can see in it a symbol of life always present on earth in the Son of whom she spoke.

Reflection Questions:

• When has water inspired you to appreciate its beauty, power or life-giving qualities?

• What have you felt refreshed when at last you reached and drank some water to slake your intense thirst?

Prayer:
Mary, Fountain of Living Water, on that Holy Mountain you stood near that fountain, reminding us that your Son is our life, the source of grace and goodness, the One sent from the Father to reconcile us back to God. You invite your children once again to come to the water that we may have life to the full.

As his first disciple, you call us to be faithful and responsive to the needs of others and thus benefit from the endless generosity of this Divine Source of Light and Life who is your Son, who lives with the Father and the Holy Spirit, one God, for ever and ever. **Amen**.

Invocation:
Our Lady of La Salette, Reconciler of Sinners, pray without ceasing for us who have recourse to you.

Chapter Twenty-Two:

When Words Become Flesh and Blood

Scripture: Matthew 23:1-12 (*The greatest among you must be your servant*)

> *Jesus told the crowds and his disciples: "The scribes and the Pharisees have taken their seat on the chair of Moses. Therefore, do and observe all things whatsoever they tell you, but do not follow their example. For they preach but they do not practice. They tie up heavy burdens [hard to carry] and lay them on people's shoulders, but they will not lift a finger to move them. All their works are performed to be seen. They widen their phylacteries and lengthen their tassels. They love places of honor at banquets, seats of honor in synagogues, greetings in marketplaces, and the salutation 'Rabbi.'*
>
> *As for you, do not be called 'Rabbi.' You have but one teacher, and you are all brothers. Call no one on earth your father; you have but one Father in heaven. Do not be called 'Master'; you have but one master, the Messiah. The greatest among you must be your servant. Whoever exalts himself will be humbled; but whoever humbles himself will be exalted.*

Reflection: A long time ago, one of the old Rabbi commentators on the Bible wrote that "he who learns but does not practice would be better off never having existed" (Sifra on Leviticus 26:3). This is a variation of the cynical rule of thumb, "Don't do what I do; do what I say." Here, "Jesus told the crowds and his disciples… 'do and observe all things whatsoever they tell you, but do not follow their example. For they preach but they do not practice.'" "They" here, are the scribes and the Pharisees, who sit on Moses' seat, and therefore, have the right and duty to teach the scriptures.

If truth be told, the pulpit saying, "practice what you preach" is not the easiest by which to abide. As a sometime-preacher, I confess having an arm's-length sympathy for those scribes and Pharisees. Not once but many times during my forays into the pulpit, I have felt that if I preached only — but only, what I actually practiced, my homiletic offerings would be brief indeed. I have often been a reluctant "pulpiteer" for the sheer fear of being shot down in mid-oratorical flight by some avenging mystical arrow. It almost happened once.

I was conducting a retreat for a large gathering of religious sisters. All had gone well. The sisters were, or seemed to be, happy with the religious wisdom that daily poured forth from my lips. I even had the temerity, at the end of the last conference, to ask the sisters "if they had any questions." Temerity indeed.

The questions touched on substance and were relatively easy to answer, until a diminutive nun sitting in the back row – don't they always sit in the back row? – raised her hand and, with all the respect she could muster, she shot this missile: "Father, do you do all you tell us to do?" "This is an excellent question," I said, struggling for time. I needed more time, so I added, "and it deserves to be answered fully and directly." I had painted myself into a corner.

This sister, I knew, was a baseball fan – nuns are the most faithful baseball fans in the world. So I decided to frame my response in baseball parlance. "Sister," I began, "on a good day, I can rack up a good average in my religious life. I manage to field some vicious ground balls and make good throws to all the bases. On such days, I am on a roll and dream of standing at the plate counting the seams on a fast ball before I hit it into the next area code. All this, of course, on a "very good day."

On other days, I couldn't see the ball even if it were served under glass. On those awful days, a ground ball would have to come with a handle for me to field it. "All in all, sister", I answered, "I really don't do all I tell you to do, but I try, and on a good day, I manage to stay off the bench."

The Lord loved everyone and he probably did not treat the scribes and Pharisees as harshly as he appears to do in the gospels. But there is one category of person he did not conceal his distaste for: the hypocrite, the person who says (or preaches) one thing and does another. The follower of Christ, according to this passage, is the person who simply preaches by doing before he or she does so in speech. In the Lord's eyes, there is no phenomenon as splendid as virtue and love that speak for themselves in real life.

At La Salette, Mary appeared in the manner and speech of her existence in heaven. There was the light of eternity that brooked no earthly shadow and there were the tears of endless grief that flowed mercifully down her face. Jesus says today that: "All the works (of the scribes and Pharisees) are performed to be seen." The Lady is seen but only by guileless children. God is her witness when she says, "*How long a time I have suffered for you! If I want my Son not to abandon you, I am obliged to plead with him constantly.*"

Her discourse is her life. Indeed, her apparition at La Salette is filled with the love, the anger, the tears, the threats, the promises, and the directness of pure passion. Looking at La Salette is a good way to learn who Mary is, what she does and how she practices the gospel command of love. She is simply a person who does what she says but also one who has become what she preaches.

Reflection Questions:

• When have you failed or chose not to practice what you preach?

• Whom do you admire for their consistent quality of practicing what they preach?

Prayer:
Mary, Mother of the Word, your life changed immediately when you became the mother of Jesus. Your faith was deepened and your blood mingled with that of God's Only Son.

As disciples of Jesus, through your intercession, we ask you to help us make our lives better likenesses to that of Jesus. May we indeed practice what we preach – all for the sake of his Kingdom. We ask this through your loving Son, who lives with the Father and the Holy Spirit, one God, for ever and ever. **Amen.**

Invocation:
Our Lady of La Salette, Reconciler of Sinners, pray without ceasing for us who have recourse to you.

Part Six:
Life, Death, and New Life

Chapter Twenty-Three:

The Bold Advances of a Loving God

Scripture: John 8:21-30 (*Jesus, the Father's Ambassador*)

Jesus said to the Pharisees: "I am going away and you will look for me, but you will die in your sin. Where I am going you cannot come." So the Jews said, "He is not going to kill himself, is he, because he said, 'Where I am going you cannot come'?" He said to them, "You belong to what is below, I belong to what is above. You belong to this world, but I do not belong to this world. That is why I told you that you will die in your sins. For if you do not believe that I AM, you will die in your sins." So they said to him, "Who are you?" Jesus said to them, "What I told you from the beginning. I have much to say about you in condemnation. But the one who sent me is true, and what I heard from him I tell the world." They did not realize that he was speaking to them of the Father.

So Jesus said (to them), "When you lift up the Son of Man, then you will realize that I AM, and that I do nothing on my own, but I say only what the Father taught me. The one who sent me is with me. He has not left me alone, because I always do what is pleasing to him." Because he spoke this way, many came to believe in him.

Reflection: A sage once said that one of the greatest duties in life, and one of the most important skills, lies in the ability to recognize the love of one's life. Recognize the "one who has been sent" to enter one's life and change it. This implies the ability to "see" as well as to seek. It implies the ability to seek as well as to cede all else in order to acquire it and keep it.

All human loves are believable. We understand the love of Romeo and Juliet. The love of husband and wife. The love of a mother for the child of her womb. These are human gifts that other humans can grasp, at least in part. But the love of God for humans, the love that gives each human person life and existence, and the love that gives each human being another kind of life is, humanly speaking, unbelievable. This love is so out of the realm of human experience that we need the help of the lover himself to grasp it fully.

Jesus said: "Where I am going you cannot come." He is going to the Father and he has invited them to join him in the love that will reign there. Refusing to believe in Jesus is, as the gospel says, the sin. "I am going away, and you will search for me, but you will die in your sin." The word "sin" is in the singular here because there is really only one sin: that of not believing in Jesus. All other sins result from this one.

Across the centuries Jesus tells the reader that between him and us there is an unbridgeable gap that only faith can negotiate. We are as unable to make that leap as the paralytic was to plunge by himself into the waters of Bethesda.

This is strengthened by the remarkable self-revelation contained in the do-or-die passage that exegetes have been pondering since the beginning: "I told you that you would die in your sins, for you will die in your sins unless you believe that I am he." This "I am he" is God's own name as given to Moses when he asked for a name from this God who would lead the Israelites out of Egypt (Exodus 3:14).

This name "I am who I am" is generally taken to mean that this is the God who was and will continue to be with God's people. To believe in Jesus is to believe in one who is present to people and constantly saves them from sin out of affection for them. He is from the Father and bears the Father's name and glory.

Faith in Christ constitutes the air and water of religion. Faith, that is, belief and trust in him as God, is the root of any relationship with him. In the course of their journey in the desert, the Israelites were bitten by poisonous serpents sent by God as punishment for speaking against God and Moses. The people repented for this sin and Moses prayed to God who told him to "make a poisonous serpent and set it on a pole; and everyone who is bitten shall look at it and live" (Numbers 21:4-9).

John refers to this when Christ tells the Pharisees that "When you have lifted up the Son of Man, then you will realize that I am he." The Son of Man lifted high on a cross will heal all those who look upon him in faith. This lifting up surely extends to the risen Christ of the resurrection as well as the Christ risen to heaven after the Ascension.

Before being healed, though, the Israelites had to repent of their sin. Then they could look up in faith and be made clean. It is ever thus in reconciliation. Faith in Christ means belief that sin, any sin, can be forgiven; that we can approach him with any pain, any disease, and he will give the hope of pardon and the healing of love. The gospel of John is indeed, a gospel of love. But this love first has to be believed.

Exaggerating only slightly, one could picture conversion of people as the everlasting dream of God. Returning to God in repentance is the constant key to growth. It is God's only avowed pleasure in heaven, to see the stray sheep and the prodigal sons and daughters coming back to the Father.

At La Salette, the Lady describes the Lord's pleasure in the Messianic abundance of the promises: "*If they are converted, rocks and stones will turn into heaps of wheat, and potatoes will be self-sown in the fields.*" And we can believe that even exaggerations can't express God's full pleasure.

Reflection Questions:
- When have you seen the light of faith grow in the heart and life

of another?

• When have you experienced reconciliation in your personal or family life or in your ministry?

Prayer:
Mary, Mother of Hope, your words on that Holy Mountain – words of rocks and stones becoming heaps of wheat, and potatoes being self-sown in the land – lift our drooping spirits and help us appreciate the promise that, if we are converted, God will reconcile us and love us into eternity.

May your words bring light to those still in darkness, food to those who hunger for the Word, life to those who have lost hope and continued strength to those who are faithful to their commitment as disciples of Jesus. We ask this through your loving Son, who lives with the Father and the Holy Spirit, one God, for ever and ever. **Amen**.

Invocation:
Our Lady of La Salette, Reconciler of Sinners, pray without ceasing for us who have recourse to you.

Chapter Twenty-Four:

The Joy of Living

Scripture: Luke 9:22-25 (*The condition of discipleship*)

Jesus said to his disciples: "The Son of Man must suffer greatly and be rejected by the elders, the chief priests, and the scribes, and be killed and on the third day be raised."

Jesus said to all: "If anyone wishes to come after me, he must deny himself and take up his cross daily and follow me. For whoever wishes to save his life will lose it, but whoever loses his life for my sake will save it. What profit is there for one to gain the whole world yet lose or forfeit himself?

Reflection: You only live when you have a purpose. I remember hearing about Niccolo Paganini (1782-1840), a famous Italian violinist and composer who owned a wonderful Stradivarius, a violin with the power to make people laugh or cry. He willed this remarkable instrument to an Italian city, with the stipulation that it never be played. The violin was displayed for all to see in an exquisite case studded with diamonds. But today, all that remains of that violin is the case. The violin itself is now a small hump of dust. Wood, if used ever so slightly, remains strong, but neglected, turns to dust.

Paganini was gifted with a silken technique, and the hands of a wizard. Seeing him play the violin, people thought him to be possessed by the devil. But Paganini had a capacity for practice that no one else could emulate. Some said that no Stradivarius was as fully exploited as his own. He was possessed by his art.

As Our Lady of La Salette reminded us in her apparition, practicing our Lenten habits of faith can strengthen our relationship with God, but it is a hands-on proposition. It reminds us that one day we will die and return to ashes. I thought I would never say that, much less write it in some public forum. It seems so sad to die, to disappear from the earth forever, to leave life.

There is something sadder than death, however, and that is to die standing up. Paganini's beautiful violin could have served another young violinist. It could have continued to make people laugh and cry for ages to come. There are many Stradivarii still playing today. Unused, they unfortunately fade away.

It gets worse. What exactly dies within us, when we avoid penance or any kind of inconvenience or hardship? Love dies, and it dies without fail, without a millisecond of doubt. Because love cannot survive without the gift of self, and there is no penance as real and as refined as the gift of self. There is no question here of an occasional, passing, act or acts of devotion. Real love is expressed over a lifetime.

No unrepentant person can love another. Love demands self-denial, and commitment to the happiness of the friend. Love is such a continuous act of devotion that it becomes a way of life, a way of being, a way of being in love. Sacrificing oneself is a bit like dying, dying to self, and, paradoxically, unless one dies in this way, one cannot truly live. There is no deep psychological or philosophic truth in all this. It is the simple currency of gospel wisdom spoken by Christ: "If any want to become my followers, let them deny themselves and take up their cross and follow me. For those who want to save their life will lose it, and those who lose their life for my sake will find it" (Matthew 16:25-26).

Sanctity always calls penance to mind, self-giving, and heroic sacrifice. Sanctity also means the incredible joy that lies out of the reach of all the languages of the world. The Preface of Lent calls this time a "joyful season". The Church reminds us of this need for self-imposed penance because it is a sign of our willingness to be forgiven and a time of spiritual exercise for the hardships of life. The joy of Lent is not meant only for the spirit or the soul.

By calling the body to penance, the Church also promises spiritual joy to the whole person. Our happiness, our ability to relate in depth with Christ and with people, to cope with life, to grow in holiness: these are the promises, and the challenges of a prayerful penance. This kind of penance is not some occasional giving up of things and comforts, it is also a taking on of commitments and responsibilities; it is an initiation into real-life living. We don't want to die standing up and we take a lesson from Paganini's violin.

Our Lady's plea for penance at La Salette does not mean that God is pleased as punch when we abstain from meat or whatever else has nothing to do with it. The idea is to give a concrete sign of reconciliation and conversion in one's life. The idea also is to practice the self-denial necessary for the conduct of a holy life of discipleship with Christ.

Some portions of the La Salette message: the incident at the farm of Coin, the stones that would be changed into "mounds of wheat", are more pleasant than others. Some, such as "they go to the butcher shop like dogs", don't fall gently on the ears, but there is as much love in one saying as in the other, and as much urgency.

Reflection Questions:
- What cross have your borne with the help of God?

- What crosses have you seen in the lives of others that have brought you to help or pray for them?

Prayer:
Mary, Cause of Our Joy, your tears of sorrow can be turned into tears of joy if we heed your words at La Salette and take up our cross and follow in the footsteps of your Son. We can only find true

life when we discover the fact that only in Christ can we find true and lasting joy.

Your challenging words concerning our need for penance simply remind us that sacrificing ourselves is necessary in order to truly live for the Lord. May your words seep into our hearts and lift us up. We ask this through your intercession and through the grace of your loving Son, who lives with the Father and the Holy Spirit, one God, for ever and ever. **Amen**.

Invocation:
Our Lady of La Salette, Reconciler of Sinners, pray without ceasing for us who have recourse to you.

Chapter Twenty-Five:

The Dying of Death

Scripture: John 8:51-59 (*Whoever keeps my word will never taste death*)

Jesus said to the Jews: "Amen, amen, I say to you, whoever keeps my word will never see death." (So) the Jews said to him, "Now we are sure that you are possessed. Abraham died, as did the prophets, yet you say, 'Whoever keeps my word will never taste death.' Are you greater than our father Abraham, who died? Or the prophets, who died? Who do you make yourself out to be?"

Jesus answered, "If I glorify myself, my glory is worth nothing; but it is my Father who glorifies me, of whom you say, 'He is our God.' You do not know him, but I know him. And if I should say that I do not know him, I would be like you a liar. But I do know him and I keep his word. Abraham your father rejoiced to see my day; he saw it and was glad.

So the Jews said to him, "You are not yet fifty years old and you have seen Abraham?" Jesus said to them, "Amen, amen, I say to you, before Abraham came to be, I AM." So they picked up stones to throw at him; but Jesus hid and went out of the temple area.

Reflection: The gospel of John leaves no doubt: Christ was a misunderstood man. Nicodemus had a difficult time understanding rebirth "from above". The Samaritan woman spoke of the water from the well and Christ spoke of "spring water gushing up to eternal life." After the miracle of the pool of Bethezda, the Jews didn't understand why Christ healed the paralytic on a sabbath. In chapter six, it says: "the Jews disputed among themselves, 'How can this man give us his flesh to eat?'" All of this was literally too good to be true.

In this gospel passage, Christ says, "whoever keeps my word will never see death." Now they really thought he had lost his sanity: "Now we know that you have a demon", they said.

In each case the enemies' misunderstanding did not concern his tactics or his politics but the saving acts he was performing. What they misunderstood was his love for them. They stuck to a mistaken perception about his mission. The love he expressed was like another language. The words he spoke were spoken by a man from another world – literally.

The revelation of this kind of love was too strong to be absorbed by the strength of ordinary humans. Hence the reason for John's strong insistence on faith throughout his gospel. He tells succeeding generations that they also could fall in the very same trap of misunderstanding the word of God in their lives.

This word does not always correspond to human logic and to the normal "common sense" sequence of human life. In some ninety-five mentions of faith, most of them in the verbal-action form of belief, John teaches that no one can believe without Christ. In weak comparison, it might be easier to climb Everest in slippers.

Then comes the revelation that "whoever keeps my word will never see death." This is really not a new revelation in John since he had already said that "everyone who believes in him may not perish but have eternal life" (John 3:16). The Christ of Saint John does not merely make the promises of love but he makes big ones, those that are bound to reach down into the very lives of men and women to eradicate from them the misery, the hopelessness that too often haunts those who walk this earth.

Death is the ultimate misery, the signal failure, the towering absurdity by which the entire population of the earth is renewed about every eighty years. Christ is not thinking of this kind of death, which we will all suffer. He is thinking of the life that comes afterward. And so people may die in their bodies, but they still exist. Death has died and life will be the final champion. This is what the coming paschal mystery will tell us in the sudden surprise of the joy of Easter morning. No wonder Christ was misunderstood.

Christ does not make things easier for the Jews when he compares himself to Abraham and declares himself prior and superior to him: "Very truly, I tell you, before Abraham was, I am." This is a clear and striking claim to divinity. This the Jews did not misunderstand. They knew what he was saying and that in their law this was nothing but blasphemy. They understood because they took up stones to throw at him.

The gifts Christ came to give were greater than the human heart's ability to grasp. Hope, joy and life are promises too great for humans to hear and to accept. At that time the Jews found it hard to believe his words. In later times we find it hard to believe his love.

At La Salette, the Lady asks that her people submit if they want to live. In the gospel, Christ says something of high moment, "Very truly, I tell you, whoever keeps my word will never see death"; that is, whoever lives in faith, believes and trusts, will not die. This certainly shows the importance of doing the will of Christ. It has a number-one priority rating since nothing is more precious than life. And only "doing his word" will gain it. The values of La Salette are all in the upper reaches of the gospel.

Reflection Questions:
- What challenges confront you about your faith, discipleship or making her message known? For what do you still need to pray?

- In what situations has the death of a believer been life-giving for you?

Prayer:
Mary, Refuge of Sinners, your deep and lasting love allows you to welcome your needy people without reserve. From your heavenly seat, you came to visit us, bringing your eternal message of forgiveness and mercy.

Continue to pray without ceasing for us and we, in turn, promise to say and do what you have requested of us in your merciful apparition. May the gospel values you mentioned become central to our faith and guide our daily life. We ask this through your intercession and through the grace of your loving Son, who lives with the Father and the Holy Spirit, one God, for ever and ever. **Amen.**

Invocation:
Our Lady of La Salette, Reconciler of Sinners, pray without ceasing for us who have recourse to you.